JOSEPH CARO

ABOUT THE AUTHOR

Joseph J. Caro is both a skilled arbitrator and mediator and has worked with and submitted changes for the "Lemon Law" (defective vehicles) program in California. Joe was the managing editor of the Route 66 Pulse – a monthly newspaper distributed in many states. A 'Car Guy' for many years and an avid writer, Joe wrote the first California "Lemon Law" book *Consumers Guide To The California Lemon Law.* Other non-technical books by Joseph include: *Collector's Guide to Hopalong Cassidy Memorabilia, Hopalong Cassidy Collectibles, On Assignment-The Great War – A photo biography of Edward N. Jackson, Santa's Christmas Train* (children's book) and *The Rainbow Butterfly* (children's book).

Joseph has written many classic car related feature articles and his photographs have appeared on the covers and within several leading magazines including:
Collector Car News, Antiques & Collecting, Drive, Pop Culture Collecting, Convertible Magazine, Reminisce, Collecting Toys, Toy Collector, Antique Trader Collector, Classic American, The Inside Collector, Down Memory Lane, Classic Auto Restorer, The Collector, That's Country, Car Collector Magazine, Antiques & Collecting, Aviation History Magazine.

Joseph lives in Huntington Beach, California with his wife Pamela.

CCN Publications

16222 Monterey Lane #104 Huntington Beach, CA 92649

Join us at: cruisin-route-66.com for news, photos and updates!

Published by CCN Publications 2015

ISBN – 10: 1518694950 ISBN – 13: 9781518694950

22.50 US   25.50 CAN

Printed in U.S.A. 2nd. edition

Front Cover - Route 66 Newberry Springs, California
Cover Design – Joseph J. Caro

Preface

Writing a biography on a person is a difficult task; what they did, where they lived, their accomplishments and friends, their family, where they came from and who they actually were is woven in a tapestry of words to bring them closer to you. When the subject that you are writing about is a key part of Americana and stretches over 2,400 miles from Chicago, to the Pacific Ocean, and is the origin of a million fond and tragic memories, and has been around, in the most part, since 1926 where do you start? What do you write about? After all, it's not an eulogy you are writing, even though the 'Grand Dame' of highways is showing her age nowadays and, for the most part, is only a shadow of her former celebrity.

Built in varying stages beginning in 1926 to transport people and families, merchandise and equipment from Chicago to the new growth communities in California and everyplace in-between, Route 66 was well suited to bear the name "Main Street U.S.A.," because in many cases, that's exactly what the road was. In the 1940's she was a place to "get your kicks on" per the lyrics of Nat 'King' Cole's popular song. In the 1960's she was a popular TV show and the filming location for many movies. Back then, Route 66 was really the only way to travel to Flagstaff, Arizona and to the Grand Canyon and most points west. Most recently, the Disney movie *Cars* brought the spotlight back to the stark emptiness associated with the closing of Route 66.Towns like 'Radiator Springs' that in reality could be Oatman, Arizona, or Seligman, Kingman, Williams, Ashfork or Peach Springs, Arizona, or a hundred others.

Personally speaking, Route 66 is simply a long ribbon of concrete and asphalt. It was the people who used it, then and now, that brought living memories from the days of the Great Depression and the Dust Bowl. People like John Steinbeck who wrote about it in the award winning *Grapes of Wrath*. People going west to a new future, or leaving an untenable past behind. The road is people and memories. It was the call of freedom that *Easy Rider* stars Peter Fonda and Dennis Hopper found, that lies in all of us. *Cruisin' Route 66* is a place and a time, both present and past, yesterday, today and tomorrow.

Let me be your guide dear reader, and show you some of my favorite places, stories and people along the way.

Joseph Caro

Foreword

Cruisin' Route 66 is a compilation of stories, facts, locations and people, a treasure trove of events and memories that I will share with you of this wonderful highway that once was, and in many cases still is, the backbone of America. I have made several trips on her during various stages of my life as have so many others. I have met wonderful people, seen wonderful sights and always enjoyed the freedom she offered me –if only for a few days or even a few hours. I have tried to include interesting places to see through my eyes and the eyes of others; current events, celebrations, restoration projects of buildings and the road itself, some uplifting stories some tragic ones; classic cars and car shows, traveler advice, and   a slice of Americana that many wish was still with us today. This wonderful road simply cannot be described with one sentence or one paragraph or one book. People that travel her byways are left with their own opinion of what they personally experienced. Your adventure awaits. You will not be disappointed.

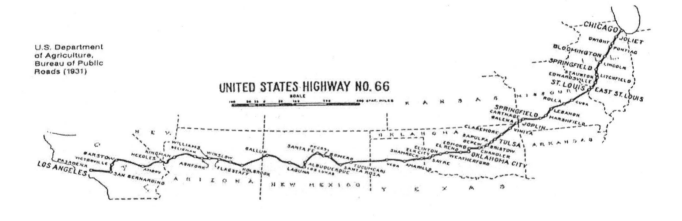

Dedication

**This book is warmly dedicated to all who have driven Route 66 in her heyday
and to those that aspire to explore her remaining beauty and driving challenge today.**

Driving Route 66 in itself, is the destination – not where it takes you

CONTENTS

"IF YOU . . . DON'T KNOW . . . WHOSE SIGNS . . . THESE ARE . . . YOU CAN'T . . . HAVE DRIVEN . . . VERY FAR . . . BURMA SHAVE!"

Route 66 was once known as "Main Street U.S.A." "The Mother Road" and to some unhappy drivers "The Mother of *ALL* Roads!" and was at one time known as the "National Trails Highway" as well as "The Will Rogers Highway." This "Grand Dame" of all highways regardless of what she was called, wended her way 2,448 miles from Adams Avenue in Chicago, Illinois (some insist it was from Michigan Avenue) all the way to Ocean Avenue in Santa Monica, California (some insist it was the Lincoln Avenue and Olympic Boulevard intersection) but I happen to prefer the Santa Monica Pier location best of all.

"HER CHARIOT . . . RACED AT . . . EIGHTY PER . . . THEY HAULED AWAY . . . WHAT HAD . . . BENHUR . . . BURMA SHAVE"

As this mostly two-lane roadway passed from the urban areas of Chicago and a few other growing towns and cities to the more rural areas where houses were few and fields, plains and deserts were a-plenty, drivers were kept entertained and often kept awake by anticipating some of the hundreds of different Burma Shave road-side jingles they would see during their travels. I personally recall reading (and loudly reciting) verses of this road-side poetry from the back seat of the family 1941 Pontiac in 1956, driving to Phoenix, Arizona to visit my grandparents. When not fighting with my brother Bob (several years my younger) or hanging my head out the side window trying to keep cool (it was July, school summer vacation – not the best time to visit Phoenix, my dad quickly found) bouncing on the back seat and singing songs only I could understand and wanting a rest stop every ten miles, I loudly repeated Burma Shave rhymes until dad could hardly stand it. By the way, after this trip the furthest vacation drive was to the Jersey shore – (we lived 50 miles away).

I soon found there was a remarkable difference between a hot July day in New Jersey and a *hot* July day in Shamrock, Texas, when we sat on the shoulder of a foot-blistering asphalt road watching a river of bubbling tar ooze from the road bed while we waited for the steaming radiator of the Pontiac to cool enough to limp to the next gas station. Mom had to slather Noxzema cream on the burnt bottoms of my feet for the next hundred miles.

"CARS IN DITCH . . . DRIVER IN TREE . . . MOON WAS FULL . . . AND SO WAS HE . . . BURMA SHAVE"

The next summer I was sent to see my grandparents in Phoenix again, by myself, in a Greyhound bus.

The Burma Shave Story

Nearly a year before Route 66 was commissioned in 1926 small wooden signs started cropping up on the shoulder of highways through many Midwestern states. The signs advertised one of the first brushless shaving creams made by a small company named Burma Shave. The first signs didn't even rhyme; "Shave the modern way –Fine for the skin." As Route 66 became more popular after WWII so did the Burma Shave signs as interest increased for their products. The company decided they had a great responsive (and cheap) advertising outlet for their products and found that drivers liked the humorous and rhyming ads best and Burma Shave learned that four or five signposts for a saying worked the best, and that drivers actually looked forward to the next set of Burma Shave signs to break the monotony of the drive:

"THIRTY DAYS . . . HATH SEPTEMBER . . . APRIL, JUNE . . . AND THE . . . SPEED OFFENDER . . .BURMA SHAVE"

There were few car radios in the early days on Route 66, and none that would receive a radio transmission from over fifty miles away. Also lacking was street lights or much else to distract a bored driver, especially at night. Burma Shave signs were the nation's first mini-billboards specifically designed to get the traveler's attention. After WWII when gasoline and tires were no longer rationed and new cars, campers and trailers were available once again, millions of people began traveling in record numbers. Running out of ideas for new slogans, Burma Shave started contests for new verses submitted from drivers themselves. Some were outright bizarre:

"RIP A FENDER . . . FROM YOUR CAR . . . MAIL IT IN . . . FOR A HALF-POUND JAR . . . BURMA SHAVE"

The company was reportedly deluged with old fenders from nearly every state! It is estimated there were over seven thousand jingles and verses at one time, but when highways turned into interstate freeways and vehicle speeds increased on well-paved roads with three and four lanes, Burma Shave slowly left the roadsides and the highway signs became historic icons of a day gone by.

"PASSING ON HILLS . . . AND CURVES YOU KNOW . . . SHOULD ONLY BE DONE . . . AT A BEAUTY SHOW . . . BURMA SHAVE"

And my favorite:

"DON'T STICK . . . YOUR ARM . . . OUT TOO FAR . . . AS IT MAY . . . GO HOME IN . . . ANOTHER CAR . . . BURMA SHAVE!

Here are a few more Burma Shave jingles to give you a chuckle:

Twinkle, twinkle . . . One-eyed car . . . We all wonder . . . WHERE you are . . . Burma-Shave

If your peach . . . Keeps out . . . Of reach . . . Better practice . . . What we preach . . . Burma-Shave

I'd heard it praised . . . By drug store clerks . . . I tried the stuff . . . Hot dog! It works . . . Burma-Shave

Spring . . . Has sprung . . . The grass has riz . . . Where last year's . . . Careless drivers is . . . Burma-Shave

Proper . . . Distance . . . To him was bunk . . . They pulled him out . . . Of some guy's trunk . . .Burma-Shave

I know . . . He's a wolf . . . Said riding hood . . . But Grandma dear, . . . He smells so good . . .Burma-Shave

Figure 1 author (r) brother Bob and Mom and our '41 Pontiac

These Wonderful Car People

These folks are a most gregarious group, whose fondness for other people is only equaled by that for the classic automobile

3

Cruisin' Route 66 - is a book about driving "The Mother Road" in your family SUV, your motorcycle or your classic ride. I do not discriminate when the subject is *what* you drive, but *where* you drive it – Route 66 of course! I have owned classic cars (and motorcycles) long before they were deemed 'classic.' I have worked on them, written about them and swore at them over the years, and found that there is a strong symbiotic relationship of the classic car to this classic road. I do not wish to slight the motoring adventurer in his modern-day vehicle from heeding the beckoning call. Far from it, Route 66 smiles at us all. There is however, something uniquely special when driving a classic vehicle on Route 66. A total emersion if you will, of mind and body, a classic vehicle (that is often older than its driver) – and "The Mother Road" herself.

Drivers come from Australia just to drive her; the Austin Club of England has traversed Route 66 hills and valleys several times, from beginning to end –shipping their classic cars beforehand. Many fly-in from Europe and rent a motorcycle just to experience "Main Street USA" often pot-holed and washboard macadam.

Cruisin' California -   California is the undisputed home of the "Hot Rod" the "Low Rider" the custom car and the dune buggy to name a few. While the first Drive-In restaurant was Kirby's Pig Stand in Dallas, Texas in 1921, and the first Drive-In movie opened in New Jersey (1933) it was Kirby's Pig Stand that had the first carhop service and led to what would become the modern day "Cruise –Nite" where teenagers would meet with their modified "rides," usually, after dark. The teenagers, are grown men now with family obligations, but still maintain a love to show their classic cars whenever they can. Welcome to Donut Derilicts – a local Huntington Beach, California donut shop that for over twenty years has been the home of the *early, early, Saturday morning cruise!* The cars start arriving at four o'clock AM!

Figure 2 early morning java

Figure 3 waiting for 6:00 am opening

4

Figure 4 concourse class Packard among hot rods

On most every day, somewhere in Southern California, you can find a car show or 'cruise nite' packed with unique vehicles to please both young and old.

Figure 5 "barn find" look is very popular

Classed as a 'rat rod' because of its deteriorated appearance, many collectors go to great lengths to achieve the above 'look.'

I have spoken with several patrons of Donut Derelicts' that arrive at 3:00AM just to insure they get a spot for their cars.

It was at Johnnie's Broiler (below) that I decided to drive Route 66 in the middle of December, and once in Chicago, continue driving to New Jersey, and then drive back to California – in a 1954 Ford.

Figure 6 Frisco's on Friday night in Downey, California

Figure 7 Johnnie's Broiler, Saturday night, Downey, California

When you drive Route 66 any time of year you can expect to find a 'cruise nite,' drive-in or car show somewhere nearby. "Car People" know the best spots to visit off of the grid, where to stay and where the best food is. You will always be welcome.

Time to "Motorvate!"

You have no doubt noticed by now that this is a West to East book on driving Route 66 principally because the relics and wide-open-spaces of the road are more east of southern California. From a practical point, if you have driven west, and are in Victorville or coming down the Cajon Pass, the only thing you have to look forward to is trying to reach the final destination of Route 66 in Santa Monica; in traffic, crowded freeways, smog and dirty air. Driving *east* however, once you are at the summit of Cajon Pass, you have clear skies, beautiful air and the most exciting and interesting parts of Route 66 lying ahead! Besides, I live in southern California not Chicago.

Santa Monica, California

Not much of Route 66 exists anyplace west of Ontario, California, but the road originally snaked through Pasadena, and then south to Los Angeles where it spent a brief time on Sunset Boulevard in Hollywood and took a final lunge to Santa Monica Boulevard through Beverly Hills to the city of Santa Monica itself. If you turn left on Lincoln Boulevard from Santa Monica Boulevard and follow it to

Olympic Boulevard you will have come to the actual end of Route 66, even though many photos (mine included) show the alternate end of this great road at Santa Monica Pier.

Figure 8 end of Route 66

In 1977 the popular song *Hotel California* alluded to Route 66 in its opening lines, "*On a dark desert highway, cool wind in my hair, Warm smell of colitas rising up through the air, Up ahead in the distance, I saw a shimmering light, My head grew heavy and my sight grew dim, I had to stop for the night*".

Figure 9 Santa Monica Pier

According to **Eagles** guitarist **Don Felder** "Everybody had driven into **Los Angeles** on what used to be Route 66. And as you drive in through the **desert** at night, you can see the glow of Los Angeles from a hundred miles away. The closer and closer you get, you start seeing all of these images, and these things pounded into our heads: the stars on **Hollywood Boulevard**, movie stars, **palm trees**, beaches and girls in **bikinis**."

If you take my suggestion and drive east, Route 66 becomes Foothill Boulevard at the interchange with SR (State Route) 210 at the base of the mountains northeast of Los Angeles in the city of La Verne. SR (State Route) 66 heads southeast for a few miles before entering Pomona and turning due east. The highway continues into the city of Claremont, passing by Claremont College, before crossing into Upland, San Bernardino County. This information is for those looking to find a needle in a haystack, as parts of '66' have become.

In Upland, SR 66 passes by Cable Airport to the south, continuing due east. The highway intersects SR 83 before entering Rancho Cucamonga, where state maintenance of SR 66 currently ends. Foothill Boulevard continues east through Rancho Cucamonga through an interchange with I-15 before entering Fontana, and passing well north of the California Speedway. (Now the AAA Speedway) Foothill Boulevard continues east into Rialto, where the SR 66 designation resumes. SR 66 continues east into San Bernardino, before curving to the north as 5th Street and terminating at I-215 south of downtown.

There is one more part of Route 66 that travels alongside I-15 up the Cajon Pass, to Victorville, but I think the majority of Route 66 fun really begins when you reach the top, at the Route 66 icon "Summit Inn." For those poor souls driving east-to-west, you have already explored the meaningful part of Route 66, now you'll be choked in traffic and smog for the next day or two trying to get to Santa

Monica. It's much more fun going *west-to-east*, you see, you have left the traffic behind and

Have nothing but blue skies and clean air ahead!

Peterson Automotive Museum

Beginning our Route 66 travels with a visit to the Petersen Automotive Museum at 6060 Wilshire Blvd. (on the corner of Wilshire Blvd. and Fairfax Street) is a great start for everything to follow. Just a few blocks south of Santa Monica Blvd. (Route 66) the Petersen Museum has recently re-opened after a 14 month, 90 MILLION dollar upgrade – and is certainly worth the $15 adult admission.

Figure 10 Petersen Automotive Museum -6060 Wilshire Blvd.

Containing some of the rarest, most exotic vehicles that were ever on the road – in reality or films; from Pebble Beach concourse show winners to 'barn finds' that made it big, there are three stories and over 95,000 square feet of exhibit space to keep you busy all afternoon.

Figure 11 1935 Bugatti 'Atlantic'

They have the 1959 Corvette XP-87 Stingray that was designed and raced by GM Bill Mitchell – the famous Mercedes W196 , 1954 Streamliner raced by the racing legends Juan-Manuel Fangio and Sterling Moss – the 1964 Aston Martin DB5 driven by James Bond in *Goldfinger.*

Figure 12 1959 Corvette Stingray

Figure 13 1954 Mercedes W196 racer

Most car lovers will recognize the founder of the museum by his name alone – Robert E. Peterson, who published *Hot Rod* magazine back in 1947 and then others, to further whet the appetite of folks who wanted more out of the iron that Detroit was building including: *Car Craft, Rod & Custom, Sports Car Graphic*, and *Motor Trend*, He also published: *CARtoons, Guns & Ammo, SPORT, Motorcyclist, Motor Life, Hunting, Mountain Biker ,Photographic, Teen, Tiger beat*, and *Sassy Magazine*. Robert "Pete" Petersen passed-away on March 23rd. 2007. Truly a 'gear head' ifthere ever was one!

The first issue of *Hot Rod* magazine, with a run of 5,000 copies, was released to coincide with the Los Angeles Hot Rod Exhibition in1947, the show Petersen and Lindsay were initially contracted to publicize. The founders sold the copies of the magazine at the steps of the exhibition

Figure 14 beautiful 'lead-sled' custom Mercury

This roadster was built to celebrate the 50th. Anniversary of the first issue of *Hot Rod* magazine as a copy of the first cover car built by Regg Schlemmer. The actual first issue of *Hot Rod* for national distribution debuted in January, 1948.

Figure 15 built in 1997 to resemble the first Hot Rod magazine cover

From custom and concept cars, race cars and rare motorcycles the Petersen Automotive Museum is certainly the place to whet your appetite for Route 66 travels. A distinctive jewel in the crown of automotive history,

Figure 16 custom Cadillac "Cadzzilla"

Figure 17 1955 Chevrolet Biscayne - concept car

Petersen's is only a few miles from the sunny beaches of Santa Monica – just a few steps from the La Brea Tar Pits – down the road a piece from Griffith Observatory- a short glittery jaunt to Hollywood - and yes, the famous Pink's hot dog stand.

La Brea Tar Pits

Located literally across the street from the Petersen Museum,(5801 Wilshire Blvd.) the La Brea Tar Pits are a group of tar pits around which Hancock Park was formed in urban Los Angeles. Natural asphalt has seeped up from the ground in this area for tens of thousands of years. The tar is often covered with dust, leaves, or water. Over many centuries, the bones of animals that were trapped in the tar were preserved.

Figure 18 ice age mammoths stuck in tar

Figure 19 amazing displays and exhibits throughout the museum

The tar is often covered with water. Over many centuries, animals that came to drink the water fell in, sank in the tar, and were preserved as bones. The museum is dedicated to researching the tar pits and displaying specimens from the animals that died there. The La Brea Tar Pits are now a registered National Natural Landmark. The museum has work rooms where you will see newly found animal bones cleaned and prepared for exhibit and study.

Griffith Park Observatory

Located in the Los Feliz area of Los Angeles, the observatory sits on the south-facing slope of Mount Hollywood. . It commands a view of the Los Angeles, basin including Downtown Los Angeles to the southeast, Hollywood to the south, and the Pacific Ocean to the southwest. The observatory is a popular tourist attraction with an excellent view of the Hollywood sign, and an extensive array of space and science-related displays. Admission is free and the planetary shows are state-of-the-art and worth the $7 for adult charge. Nearby places of interest is the Los Angeles Zoo and the Gene Autry Museum.

Figure 20   2800 E. Observatory Rd. Los Angeles

A stones throw from the glitter of Hollywood and a scenic drive through Beverly Hills, Griffith Observatory was used as a movie location set in a number of films including: Rebel Without a Cause –The Rocketeer – The Terminator – Transformers- Earth Girls are Easy – Agent Carter – Charlie's Angels Full Throttle, and many, many more. Griffith Park covers more than 4,107 acres of natural terrain. Located right in the middle of Los Angeles, it is one of the largest municipal parks in the United States. The Park is so big and has so many things to do that it's hard to think of it as a "park." At least not like the one down the street with a slide, swings and two picnic tables. If you plopped it down in San Francisco, its 6 square miles would cover one-eighth of the city. It's five times larger and far more untamed than New York City's Central Park.

Some things to do in Griffith Park are manmade, like the zoo and museums and historic train rides.

Hollywood, California

Downtown Hollywood today is little more than a glitzy tourist magnet filled with maps-of-the-stars- homes mentality. If you want to have fun without taking what you see too seriously, you too can visit The' Boulevard of Stars' and go to what was once Grumman's Chinese Theatre and see just how big Gary Cooper's footprints really were.

The other side of the hill (Studio City) will take you to Universal Studios and the Universal City Walk for thrilling touristy entertainment.

Figure 21 twilight on Hollywood Blvd.

If you want to do something quite unique in Hollywood, drive into the hills on Beachwood Drive, (under the Hollywood sign) rent a horse at the stables there, and ride the trails east to Griffith Park. The Magic Castle on Fountain Ave. is a great experience – but you have to be invited by a member to visit there, or stay at the Magic Castle hotel.

Pink's Hot Dogs

I only venture to Hollywood when necessary these days – (I lived near town on Beachwood Drive for several years) but one thing that still attracts me here is –Pink's hot dogs!

Pink's was founded by Paul and Betty Pink in 1939 as a pushcart near the corner of **La Brea** and **Melrose**. The **Great Depression** was still having an impact on the country, and money was scarce. People could purchase a **chili dog** made with Betty's own chili recipe accompanied by mustard and onions on a steamed bun for 10 cents each. As business grew, thanks to Betty's chili and the custom-made Hoffy-brand hot dogs with their natural **casings**, so did Pink's. The family built the current building in 1946 at 709 north La Brea Ave.

Figure 22 Pink's hot dogs -Melrose and La Brea

Orson Wells was said to be such a fan of Pink's – he would pull-up to the curb in his limo and eat as many as 12 Pink's chili dogs before he left. I have frequented Pink's for many years and two chili dogs is my limit. That was when car clubs would 'cruise' Hollywood. and Sunset Blvd. Cruisin' Hollywood is a big no- no today.

Ontario, California

Figure 24 specially built 66"Special"

Figure 23 classic Ford "high boy"

16

One of the biggest, baddest car shows in Southern California is the Ontario "Cruisin' Reunion" held on Euclid Avenue, Ontario several blocks from Foothill Boulevard (Route 66). This is a Sunday event, but pre-1975 classic cars start arriving on Saturday. The 2015 event should bring over 1,200 classic cars and 300,000 spectators.

Figure **25** custom 1956 Cadillac

Figure 26 Starbuck's on Foothill Blvd.

Figure 27 Ontario Car Show - 2006

CHAPTER
TWO

Mysteries and Ghosts

On Route 66

Before we continue on our driving adventure we may want to explore the ethereal nature of the "Old Road" that may 'haunt' many travelers.
We all like a good scary story from time to time and Route 66 has more than its share to give you a good case of the 'willies.' Some are funny, others scary and some are just plain weird! If the 1970 song by the Eagles, *Hotel California* was written about driving to Los Angeles, California on Route 66 back then, it could give some a good case of shivers today with the following lyrics: . . .

Last thing I remember, I was running for the door, I had to find the passage back to the place I was before."Relax "said the night man, we are programmed to receive. You can check-out any time you like. But you can never leave!

Here are but a few of the many Route 66 related stories that never leave:

Oatman Hotel

There are several old hotels along Route 66 that have maintained a reputation of ghostly apparitions including the Oatman Hotel in Oatman, Arizona, which is one of the biggest attractions because of the reportedly celebrity ghosts of Clark Gable and Carole Lombard. Many guests and staff members claim to have often heard whispering and laughing from the Gable and Lombard honeymoon room when it is empty. According to one report, when a photographer took a picture of the empty room, the ghostly figure of a man appeared on the developed print.

There are other spirits that reportedly haunt the old Oatman Hotel. The second floor houses a Theater Room Museum where distinct outlines and impressions of sleeping bodies have been found in the dust on the beds. Upon closer inspection, none of the surrounding areas appear to be disturbed. Staff suspects that the sleeping spirit is that of a former, long deceased chambermaid who had often been spotted in the room. Then there is the story about "Oatie," the ghost of an Irish miner that died in an Oatman hotel room and has haunted the place ever since. He is often heard playing his bagpipe around the hotel – in the dead of night. Other common pranks "Oatie" indulges in include opening and slamming shut the window in his former room and pulling the covers off of the bed. There are also reports of the room being very cold – in the midst of a hot desert day.

The Needles Triangle

I call this area "The Needles Triangle" . . . the juncture of California, Arizona and Nevada. Similar to the Bermuda Triangle off the Florida coast, there are many reported UFO sightings in this tri-state area.

The Devil's Highway

Many impressionistic travelers claim that the Route 66 part of Highway 666 also has its share of devilish apparitions:

Route 666 is a lonely, deserted stretch of road with a long history of accidents and ghosts and unexplained events. Because of the so-called bad luck along this stretch of road, highway officials in all four states maintaining the "666" road have been asked to change the name of this highway. Most have relented, including Arizona, which now lists it as Highway 191. What does this have to do with the "Mother Road" you may ask? It is reported that Route 666 originally was the sixth branch of the now defunct Route 66, in that state, and therefore became Route 666. (The sixth branch of Route 66?) New maps may list this road as Highway 191 . . . but the old maps will show you the locations of the demonic highway called "Route 666."

Devil Trucker

One popular story of "Route 666" is about a "Devil Trucker" as reported by a man whom when driving this road at night states that he saw a truck that looked like it was on fire, and heading straight for him from the opposite direction, right down the middle of the highway. The truck was going so fast, the man claims, that sparks were flying off the wheels and flames were coming from the smokestack [exhaust stack]. He claimed that this apparition scared him so bad that he pulled off the road and ran 20 feet out into the open desert away from his car and waited for the truck to pass. He claims that the truck passed him at over 120 mph, and that the truck was glowing red.

Route 666 Devil Dogs

Reported packs of "Devil Dogs" seemingly roam all parts of Highway 666 and attack cars, trucks and campers in the dead of night. They have glow-in-the-dark bright yellow eyes and long, sharp fangs used to shred the tires of any traveler silly enough to stop on the side of this haunted road.

The Ghostly Trans Am

One Route 66 favorite ghost story follows the motoring death of Sam Kinison, the comedian/ actor who died in a solo car crash on old Route 66 near Needles, California in 1992. Locals say they sometimes glimpse Kinison's white Trans Am racing on that stretch of deadly road, followed by the sound of screeching brakes and crashing metal, in the middle of the night. When they look for accident debris, the road is empty.

Route 66 travelers driving thru Missouri may want to get a copy of *Missouri's Haunted Route 66* to keep them company or, *Haunted Highway: The Spirits of Route 66*.

Route 66 travelers who relish Goosebumps and sleepless nights while exploring the "Old Road" would undoubtedly enjoy stories about the "Spook Light," near Quapaw, Oklahoma, and the haunted Hotel Monte Vista in Flagstaff, Arizona, that boasts so many ghost stories it has devoted a section of its website where you will find the apparitions of a bank robber, several prostitutes, a bellboy, a baby, a dancing couple, and "The Meat Man." The hotel states that Room 305 is its "most active" in terms of paranormal activity, and includes an empty rocking chair that rocks by itself.

Legend has it that along Route 66 between Weatherford and El Reno, Oklahoma the ghost of an old, humpbacked man is often spotted. He wears a fedora and a trench coat and is most often seen on rainy or foggy nights. Some describe the man as a "phantom rider" or the "vanishing hitch-hiker" that will wave a driver down for a ride, won't speak to the helpful driver at all, then after several miles, this strange passenger suddenly attempts to leap from the vehicle. When the driver stops the car to let him out, the ghostly hitch-hiker has vanished. Shaken by this ghostly apparition, the frightened driver then sees the same man again, walking along the road – several miles ahead. Another legend recounts how a driver thinks he had just struck an elderly man as he was crossing the road, but when the driver gets out, the injured man is nowhere to be seen.

Barney's Beanery

If you are driving to the end of Route 66, you should stop at the famous Barney's Beanery, a fixture on old Route 66 in West Hollywood, California (8447 Santa Monica Blvd.) Barney's is known for many things: home of the Second-Best Chili in Los Angeles; the one-time hangout for Janis Joplin, Jim Morrison ("The Doors" lead singer), and scads of other music artists and movie stars. . . and the ghostly "roof-top man" trampling across the top floor of the beanery, that some insist is the ghost of Jim Morrison.

Another Missouri spooky favorite is the now closed Tri-County Truck Stop, Villa Ridge, MO. which has been investigated by Missouri Paranormal Research after reports of strange activity and apparitions.

Stories continue to prevail about the legendary "Ghost Bridge" of Route 66 in Lincoln, Illinois and hundreds of stories just like it.

UFO Crashes on Route 66

Certainly not to be slighted, Route 66 has many reports of UFO sightings in the clear night desert sky. In 2008 there was a reported UFO crash outside of Needles, California that was so newsworthy a film crew came from Europe to do a story about Route 66, the "Needles Triangle" and the UFO crash, according to the local paper, the Mohave Daily News. Those who saw the UFO descending, claim that it was a fiery turquoise color and traveled across the sky at great speed. Any thought of the object being a meteorite was quickly dismissed because shortly following the sighting, many military helicopters arrived, searching for the UFO. Eyewitnesses claimed that several of the helicopters eventually located the object, and moved it to an unknown location.

One cynical witness however, stated: "I reckon it was an experimental military drone aircraft — like the ones used in Pakistan against al-Qaida and the Taliban — that wandered too far from a nearby (military) base during test flights. I certainly don't think it was from outer space."

If we drive the I-15 up the Cajon Pass we will sail past Victorville, California and glimpse the famous Summit Inn on the right. Victorville is the home of the Route 66 Museum and is on the "Old Road 66." Both are worth the time to visit.

The present location of Summit Inn (1953) is on the right of the northbound I-15 at the summit of the Cajon Pass. The original Summit Inn (1928) was located between the north and southbound lanes of Route 66 and was moved to its present location when Route 66 was rerouted.

Figure 28   Summit Inn off I-15 top of Cajon Pass

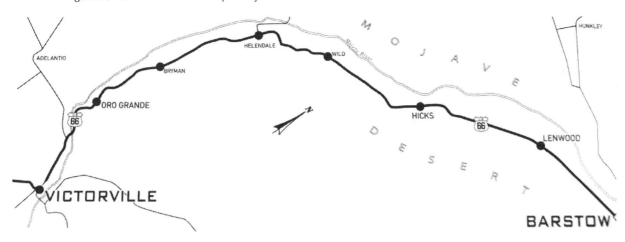

Victorville, California

Figure 29 don't miss the Route 66 Museum

If you drive through Victorville to summit the Cajon Pass you may want to stop at the Route 66 Museum on "D" street which was the old Route 66 highway winding down the high plateau to San Bernardino. There are many original Route 66 artifacts at the museum and friendly people happy to explain them, like the old Auto Club sign on the previous page.

Calico Ghost Town

Calico is a restored ghost town and former **mining town** in **San Bernardino County**; Located in the Calico Mountains of the **Mojave Desert** region of **Southern California**. It was founded in 1881 as a silver mining town, and today has been converted into a county park named *Calico Ghost Town*. Located off **Interstate I-15**, Calico lies 3 miles from **Barstow** and 3 miles from **Yermo**. It is actually adjacent to Route 66 and is fun to visit.

Giant letters spelling *"CALICO"* on the **Calico peaks** behind the ghost town can be seen from the freeway. **Walter Knott** (founder of "Knott's Berry Farm" amusement park and the "Knott's" line of jams and jellies sold in most stores) purchased Calico in the 1950s, architecturally restoring all but the five remaining original buildings to look as they did in the 1880s. Calico was designated **California Historical Landmark #782.**

Figure 30 downtown Calico

Figure 31 lady poses in handcuffs, with the headless sheriff

There are many activities at Calico for the entire family including panning for gold, a mining train tour of the town, a Saturday night ghost tour, cowboy shoot-outs on Main Street and a two hour tour of the Silver King mine. There are several restaurants and a potpourri of various shops.

Calico Ghost Town offers 265 camping sites with accommodations for RV's with full and partial hook-ups as well as group tent camping sites. The campgrounds offer hot showers, restrooms, grills and fire rings and two dump stations. Campsites are available near OHV areas of the park.

Enjoy your stay at Calico because you trip on Route 66 may become a lot more basic.

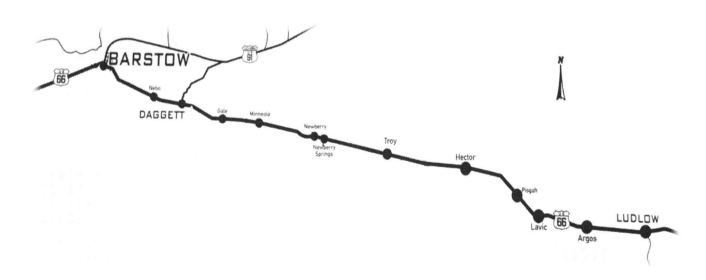

Perhaps the most original, undisturbed and largest section of Route 66 (157 miles) reaches from Newberry Springs, California (near Barstow) to Seligman, Arizona. (or the other way around –if you are traveling west) replete with ghost towns, abandoned businesses, several extinct volcano's and lava fields, closed silver and gold mines, places to explore, lost towns and treasures. Rumors of huge veins of silver and big gold nuggets in adjacent hills still prevail. And sightings of ghosts of miners and residents and victims of deadly accidents have been reported. Driving out here where nights are filled with a million stars and time has seemingly stood still for a million years, you may find yourself humming snatches of the Bobby Troup song: *Get Your Kicks* or maybe lyrics from *Hotel California*.

Newberry Springs, California

20 miles on I- 40 east of Barstow, you will find the turn-off to Newberry Springs- and the first actual sight of a good stretch of old Route 66 (if you are traveling east.) Just a few miles down this part of "The Mother Road" will take you to the famous Bagdad Café, on the left side of the road, looking as out of place as an "A" frame cabin would, in the middle of the desert.

Figure 32 Bagdad I attracts classic cars from every state

Figure 33 the Bagdad is famous for its buffalo burger

Bagdad Cafe

Next to the Bagdad Café you will see the remaining foundation of what was the motel also made famous in the 1987 film *Bagdad Café* directed by Percy Adlon and starring Marianne Sagebrecht and Jack Palance. The film is also known as *Out of Rosenheim* (German) an award winning film in Europe (7 awards) German tourists have been known specifically to go out of their way to visit the site. Unfortunately, the water tank that was featured in the film was blown down several years ago and destroyed.

Figure 34   in 1986 I often stopped here, when it was called the Sidewinder Cafe in my classic 250-S Mercedes

The town of Bagdad, California is situated near Amboy, quite a few miles east of the Café used in the film (originally called the Sidewinder Café) and is a bare spot on the road today. You no longer can safely drive much past Newberry Springs because of the condition of the road itself and the lack of minimal maintenance by the state of California.

There was an actual Bagdad that existed in the 1960s when U.S. Route 66 ran through the town. The town of Bagdad included a café, a gasoline station, cabins for rent, and an airstrip. When Interstate 40 opened and bypassed the two-lane Route 66, the town's economy collapsed and the businesses all

closed; eventually the town was completely razed. It is marked today by a clearing on the north side of old Route 66 and a single tree. If you have a chance to see the film before you visit the Bagdad Café, you will thank me for it.

My '57 Chevy did *not* take kindly to the road disrepair past Bagdad Café. I was forced to drive the dirt shoulder. Several years ago I could have driven to Ludlow without a problem (on the road-not the shoulder).

Ludlow, California

Ludlow began life as a water stop for the Atlantic and Pacific Railroad in 1883. Silver ore was found in the nearby hills, leading to a boom. From 1906 to 1940 it was the southern railhead for the Tonopah and Tidewater Railroad, operated by the Pacific Coast Borax Company that brought borax and other mining products from Death Valley and Beatty, Nevada to the Santa Fe Railway lines for national use.

By the 1940s, local mining had played-out and railway activity had declined and the town survived supplying the needs of travelers on the National Old Trails Highway, renamed to become the legendary Route 66 in California. Ludlow had a Motor Court and cabins, the Ludlow Cafe, a gasoline-service garage, and shade and water to service a barren stretch of Route 66. The town of Ludlow finally closed its doors after Interstate 40 was built in the mid-70's bypassing the town completely. Interesting note: many of the old railroad workers cabins were made from railroad ties because building wood was nearly impossible to find. Many empty buildings and Tamarisk trees still stand flanking the old highway with an old cemetery. There is a modern gas station and mini-mart adjacent to I-40.

Figure 35 Mercantile Co – 1908

Figure 36   cabins made from railroad ties

Figure 37   many buildings ready to collapse

Figure 38   Ludlow cemetery

Figure 39 Ludlow Cafe

The buildings in Ludlow are pretty much standing and a visitor may roam most of them. Care should be taken because many are unstable. The Ludlow Hotel is no longer standing and once was a known speak-easy for railroad workers.

Figure 40 my '57 Chevy didn't like the road

Because of its completeness and history, Ludlow should be considered as a state park and protected from vandalism and restored to a 1950's era at the height of its popularity. Having a hotel that once was a speak-easy-and a house of prostitution only ads character to this desert ghost town.

The road is so poorly maintained that I was forced to drive the shoulder from Newberry Springs. I still had to take I-40 most of the way to Ludlow. As little as ten years ago, the road was very drivable.

Figure 41 many abandoned homes ready to collapse

Goffs, California

Figure 42   welcome to Goffs –pop 23

Goffs (population 23) is a town I found purely by accident while exploring a few drivable roads off Route 66. It is an old railroad town (like Ludlow was) but has somehow kept from being abandoned after Route 66 re-aligned around it in 1931.

Goffs is accessible from Interstate 40 at Highway 95 north. A left turn onto Goffs Road becomes a desolate forty-mile (64 km) stretch that served as home to several towns that have mostly vanished, including Bannock, Ibis, and Homer. Continuing west on Goffs Road brings motorists back to I-40 northeast of the town of Essex.

Figure 43   giant pulley wheels were used for mining

I have visited Goffs several times and never found the General Store open for business. A remarkably clean town but I never found any people there.

Figure 44   Goffs general store

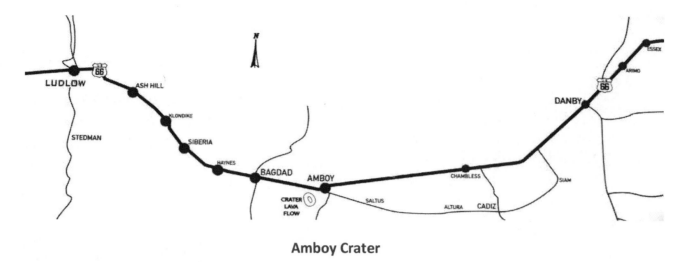

Amboy Crater

Amboy Crater and **Lava Field** is an **extinct North American cinder cone** type of **volcano** that rises above a 27 sq mile **lava field** . You can still see chunks of lava for miles as you drive Route 66 towards Amboy. It is located about 75 miles between **Barstow** to the west and **Needles** to the east, and is in the desert about 2.5 miles southwest of Route 66 , which you can clearly see when you near the town of Amboy. The volcano is said to have formed over 79,000 years ago.

The scenic and solitary Amboy Crater was a popular sight-seeing stop for travelers on **U.S. Route 66 in California** before the opening of **Interstate 40** in 1973. Other than a stretch of **U.S. Route 66 in New Mexico**, Amboy Crater was one of few extinct volcanoes along the entire route, so generations of U.S. Route 66 travelers from the 1920s through the 1960s could boast that they had climbed a real **volcano**. Visits decreased after I-40 opened, but have increased in recent years with the nearby **Mitchell Caverns, Mojave National Preserve** , and renewed historical tourism interest in "old Route 66." The crater is a few miles west of Roy's Café, and you can hike over and climb it if you want, but be careful of things that bite!

There are several extinct volcanos along Route 66 before you reach the Amboy Crater (now a state historical park) and I counted at least six.

Figure 45   this is *NOT* the Amboy Crater

Figure 11 this also, is *NOT* the Amboy Crater

THIS *is* the Amboy Crater

Figure 12 this *IS* the Amboy Crater Note the lava in foreground

Roy's Café, Amboy, California

In 1938, Roy Crowl opened Roy's as a gas and service station along the legendary U.S. Highway 66 in Amboy. At the time, Route 66 was the primary east-west highway artery crossing the nation from Chicago and the southwest to Los Angeles. The construction of Roy's was a consequence of the Route 66 realignment through Mountain Springs Summit, bypassing Goffs to directly connect Needles and Essex, and continuing west to Amboy.

Figure 13 Roy's Cafe, Amboy, CA

In the 1940s, Crowl teamed up with his son-in-law, Herman "Buster" Burris. They expanded the business, as Roy's Motel and Café, to include a café, an auto repair garage, and an auto court comprised of small cabins for overnight rental by Route 66 travelers. Buster Burris himself almost singlehandedly created the town's infrastructure, some of which remains semi-functioning today. Burris even brought power to Amboy and Roy's all the way from Barstow by erecting his own poles and wires alongside Route 66 using an old Studebaker pickup truck.

Postwar business boomed as families discovered the joys of motor travel after the World War II years of tire and gasoline rationing and the advent of new cars being built once again. Roy Crowl and Burris kept Roy's Garage and Café operating 24 hours a day – seven days a week; so busy was Roy's that Burris took out classified ads in newspapers across the country in the hope of recruiting help.

By the opening of the 1950s, Roy's complex employed up to 70 people; the town's entire population was 700 at that time.

Actors Harrison Ford and Anthony Hopkins have autographed photos on the restaurant's wall, and often visited when filming schedules allowed. Ford frequently flew in, landing his plane on a nearby landing strip reportedly, one of the first air strips in California.

Part of the 1986 motion picture *The Hitcher* with **Rutger Hauer** was filmed in Amboy. Both the reception area and neon sign helped establish the setting for a 1999 television commercial. In September 1993, *Kalifornia* was released, starring Brad Pitt, which was also filmed in Amboy. Roy's is a natural stopping area for those riding the "Old Road" west from Laughlin, Nevada and Lake Havasu City Arizona.

Figure 14 Roy's was a perfect rest stop for travelers going and coming from the casinos at Laughlin, NV before the state closed Route 66 into Chambless and all points east

Figure 15 Model 'T' truck in Chambless

Chambless, California

Chambless is a ghost town in the Mojave Desert south of Interstate 40 on Route 66. The town is east of the Bullion Mountains and Ludlow and ten miles east of Amboy Crater and Amboy, California.

While Chambless is no longer a town, in the eyes of the state of California, there were several homes and businesses occupied here several years ago. I especially liked the famous Palo Verde shoe tree –a side-of-the-road tree blooming with pairs of shoes on most all of its branches. The abandoned "Road Runner Retreat" is probably the last standing reminder of a bygone era and can be seen several miles past the "Road Closed" sign.

Figure 16 defunct Road Runner Retreat

There is a lot of reported history in the Chambless area . . .if you can find it, but much of it may be buried in the all encompassing desert sand. During WWII, General George S. Patton ran his Desert Training Center south of Chambless, with hundreds of tanks and support vehicles- trucks and motorcycles to train his 20,000 troops. His plan was to take North Africa and defeat General Erwin Rommell, Hitler's "Desert Fox." Patton trained thousands of troops in this arid land, encompassing 10,000 square miles.

The persuasive rumor today is that when Patton left with his troops his orders were to do so in a hurry . . . so he buried hundreds of tanks and other support vehicles in the desert sand! And according to rumor, they are still there

Figure 17 another Chambless relic of better days

Figure 18 Needles, California

Needles, California

Originally a tent town for railroad construction crews, the railroad company built a hotel, car sheds, shops and a roundhouse. Within a month the town also boasted a Chinese washhouse, a newsstand, a restaurant, a couple of general stores, and nine or ten saloons. The town became the largest port on the Colorado River above Yuma, Arizona. Needles was a major stop on the historic U.S. Route 66highway from the 1920s through the 1960s. For immigrants from the Midwest Dust Bowl in the 1930s it was the first town that marked their arrival in California. The city is lined with motels and other shops from that era.

The "Carty's Camp" which appears briefly in *The Grapes of Wrath,* as the Joad family enters California from Arizona is now a ghost tourist court, its remains located behind the 1946-era 66 Motel. Crossing the nearby Colorado River heading east, puts you in Arizona and a few short miles from Laughlin, Nevada Casinos, Lake Havasu City, Bullhead City, Arizona and the old Route 66 going to Oatman, Arizona.

Figure 19 Colorado River

Figure 20 Topock Arch Bridge

Topock, Arizona

Topock lies between Bullhead City and Lake Havasu City and southeast of Needles, California, on the California–Arizona border.

Topock is known for being a boating town as well as for being home to the Old Trails Arch Bridge which used to be the old Route 66 bridge featured in the film –*The Grapes of Wrath.* The crossings of the Colorado River at Topock, including the Old Trails Arch Bridge, are prominently featured in the opening scenes of the movie *Easy Rider.*

Topock Marina is located just off I-40 on Historic Route 66. It is situated on the Colorado River between Needles and Lake Havasu City, the Marina is the traditional refueling point for boaters traveling between these two cities.

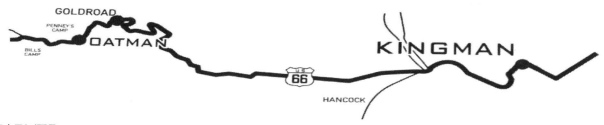

CHAPTER
THREE

Figure 21 Route 66 to Oatman, AZ off of I-40

Figure 22 two residents of Oatman

Oatman, Arizona:

'A Town Too Mean To Die'

Once a thriving gold mining town that went bust – once a major stop on old Route 66 that was closed for being too dangerous to travel, Oatman has not only remained intact in the isolated Black Mountains but has become a destination day-trip, thanks to the casino boom in Laughlin, Nevada, several miles away. "In The Middle of Things" as stated in the Chamber of Commerce brochure, Oatman is 25 miles from Kingman, AZ, 25 miles from Needles, CA – a mere 60 miles from Lake Havasu, Arizona and only 30 miles from the Colorado River and the casino night-life at Laughlin, Nevada.

Access to Oatman is by a winding, narrow two-lane road on the west, and a road that has the distinction of being the most dangerous on Route 66 going to Kingman, Arizona. Driving east over Mine Summit, (Sitgreaves Pass) Route 66 is comprised of switch-back roads, no lights and no side road barriers and reportedly the most accident prone part of old Route 66 that was closed and by-passed in 1956. Night travel to get there even today is discouraged. Stories are that in the 1920's the road from Kingman, was so steep many vehicles could only make the summit by driving up the steep grade in reverse!

The first thing you will find when you arrive in Oatman is the seemingly endless assortment of wild burrows everywhere you look (especially in the street). These animals are reportedly descendents of prospector's burrows that were abandoned when the town stopped producing gold in the mid-1920's. Living in the surrounding hills, the burrows come to town every day happily hustling drivers to pay a toll (mainly carrots) to let them drive by -and will often block road traffic till they get their fill.

The omnipresent burrow however, is loved by all residents, so never blow your horn at them! Oatman is also known as the home of the International Burro Biscuit Throwing Contest with events on an almost daily basis.

Figure 23 he may look full of carrots, but won't let you by 'till you feed him some!

Dollar Bill Bar—Oatman Hotel. During the 1920's, the story goes, a local gold miner that frequented the Oatman Hotel bar most evenings, gave the bartender a handful of dollar bills on Friday, when he was paid, so he would always have a drinking reserve. The bartender would tape them to the back bar with his name written on each, to be redeemed when needed.

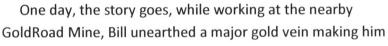

One day, the story goes, while working at the nearby GoldRoad Mine, Bill unearthed a major gold vein making him

Figure 24 famous "Dollar Bill" bar

a very rich man. Other miners started taping dollar bills to the bar walls in hopes they too would get lucky in the gold fields. The tradition continues today, to the joy of the bar owner.

The Oatman Hotel itself is the source of Hollywood celebrity when acting star Clark Gable and Carole Lombard honeymooned there when he was filming *"Gone With the Wind."* Gable and Lombard decided to solidify their steamy romance and they drove to Kingman, Arizona for a secret wedding ceremony out of the public eye.

After their return drive up the dangerous road from Kingman to Mine Summit and Oatman that night, they decided to check-in at the Oatman Hotel. The room they stayed in has been kept as a memorial to the star-crossed lovers, replete with all the original furniture to this day. Management will let you view it, but not stay in it.

Figure 25 Gable-Lombard room

It's a short drive from Oatman to Laughlin, Nevada, often called "Baby Vegas" on the banks of the Colorado River where you can get a room for a tenth what you would pay in Las Vegas. As a matter-of-fact, I was staying at Harrah's Casino when the biker gangs of the 'Hells Angels' and the 'Mongol's' decided to mix it up on the casino floor. The ensuing shoot-out was reminiscent of the old 'wild west' days! I do like Laughlin as

Figure 26 "Colorado Belle Casino, Laughlin, NV

an oasis in the desert regardless of its adventurous past, and I can't say I won at the casinos there, but enjoyed my stay none-the-less. Like br'er rabbit from Disney's hit film *"Song of the South"* (1946) I calls Laughlin, Nevada "my laffin' place!"

Figure 28miners shack in GoldRoad

Figure 29 an actual GoldRoad miner

If you continue north on Route 66 you will see miner's shacks throughout the hills north of Oatman. When you come to the crest of the road you will be at Sitgreaves Pass (Mine Summit) with a view of the GoldRoad mines, many of which are still functioning. This is the most dangerous road on all of Route 66.In the distance is Kingman, Arizona. If you look closely, you will see the carcasses of wrecked vehicles throughout the Black Mountain area.

The view from the top of Sitgreaves Pass (3,500') is worth a photo opportunity on a clear day.

As you drive down the road toward Kingman, you will come to the totally rebuilt Cool Springs Service Station that was originally constructed in the 1920's and eventually added a bar and cabins. When Route 66 bypassed this area in 1936, the station struggled on, but finally closed in 1964. The remaining structures were blown-up during a scene in the 1991 Dolph Lundgren/Jean-Claude Van Damme film *Universal Soldier.*

Figure 30 Sitegraves Pass view

Figure 31 miners shacks near Goldroad

Old and new "Cool Springs" station at Sitgreaves Pass on Route 66. Ed's Camp is a mile or two further down this windy part of Route 66 which eventually enters Kingman, Arizona.

Figure 33"Cool Springs" addition, signed in 1956

Figure 34 new "Cool Springs" tourist area – recently rebuilt as it originally stood. A great view with lots of interesting visitor items

CHAPTER FOUR

Lake Havasu City, Arizona

Before we proceed from Oatman- to- Kingman, Arizona as shown on the map above, I will ask you to make a little detour with me and amble *back* through Oatman, all the way to I-40 *west* to highway 95. I ask this for several reasons; you were probably going to visit the casinos at Laughlin, Nevada anyway – and I want to take you to Peach Springs, which is north of Kingman on a beautiful part of Route 66 – Also, I don't want you to miss "The "Globe" *and* (the real reason) there is the "Run To The Sun" car show in Havasu today, and I know you don't want to miss it! Besides, it's only 60 miles away.

The principal tourist attraction in Lake Havasu City is the **London Bridge,** which crosses a narrow channel that leads from **Lake Havasu** (a segment of the **Colorado River**) to Thompson Bay (also on the **Colorado River**). It was bought for US $2.5 million from the **City of London** when the bridge was replaced in 1968. The bridge was disassembled, and the marked stones were shipped to Lake Havasu City and reassembled for another US $7 million. It opened on October 5, 1971.

Figure 35 London Bridge and Lake Havasu

Figure 36 London Bridge

Technically, Lake Havasu City is not on Route 66 – it's on I-95 south of I-40 between Needles, California and Kingman. If you like to boat or fish, Havasu is an oasis in the desert. Every year in October they host the weekend-long car show starting on Friday to Sunday. Exhibitors come from at least four states to attend. 'Cruise Nite' was on Friday, the formal show was Saturday. Photos are from the 'cruise nite.'

Figure 38 hundreds of classic cars

Figure 37 original 1953 Mercury

I wanted to stay all weekend, but the show was full and not taking additional registrations. Both my 1957 Chevrolet and I, sadly left Havasu – to continue our odyssey for special places to visit on Route 66. So back to Kingman on I-40 so we can visit "The Globe."

Figure 39 many cars were brought here in trailers

Kingman, Arizona

There are two ways to drive to Kingman, Arizona from Lake Havasu City and I suggest going north on I-95 until you reach I-40 (about thirty miles) and taking I-40 east to Kingman. Keep your eye peeled for this marvelous structure on the right side which, according to its signage, is on Route 66, a stone throw from I-40.

Figure 40 I call it "The Globe" and was located in the middle of nowhere -20 years ago and it was for sale.

Someone had obviously purchased "The Globe" built a mini-mart in the background and may even live in "The Globe" itself. While it was for sale in the 80s, it seems to be for sale again, as there is a large 'For Sale' banner attached to another on site building. Although tempting, I did not stop to inquire about it . . . my wife would never let me live there.

You can see Route 66 in the below photo foreground.

Figure 41 "The Globe" and mini-mart

Kingman, Arizona

Lt. Edward Fitzgerald Beale, a U.S. Navy officer in the service of the U.S. Army Corps of Topographical Engineers, was ordered by the U.S. War Department to build a federal wagon road across the 35th Parallel. His secondary orders were to test the feasibility of the use of camels as pack animals in the southwestern desert. (Did you see the movie *Hawmps* starring James Hampton and Slim Pickens 1976 release?) Beale traveled through Kingman in 1857 surveying the road and in 1859 to build the road. The road became part of Route 66 and then was bypassed by the 'adjusted' safer segment of Route 66 in 1953. Remnants of the wagon road can still be seen in White Cliffs Canyon in Kingman. They scrapped the idea of using camels as pack animals as portrayed in the comedy film *Hawmps*.

Figure 42 there is much to see in Old Town Kingman on Route 66

Figure 43 this is the railroad museum . . . you should go, plenty to see and do.

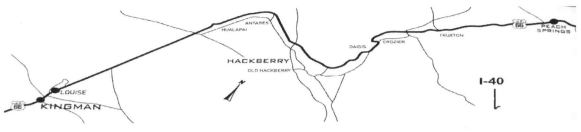

Hackberry, Arizona

"Don't blink –You'll miss us!"

A former mining town, Hackberry was named by the first inhabitants, Charles Cummings (Cummings Ranch). The name "Hackberry" was from the pellets or matting's that gathered on the cattle's long hair, probably caused from burrs picked up from bushes in the area.

Prospector Jim Music helped develop the Hackberry Silver Mine in 1875. Mining of various metals developed the town, sending it from boom to bust based on fluctuating commodity prices. Hackberry is 23 miles north of Kingman on Route 66.

Figure 44 truck has seen better days

Figure 45 old and tired - but still a treasure to somebody

Figure 46 the Hackberry General Store

The drive on Route 66 that loops up to Peach Springs and then descends to Seligman is by far, the most beautiful countryside that I've seen anywhere on Route 66. The road on this loop is as good if not better than I-40, with air so sweet you can taste it! Believe it or not, there are still quite a few Burma Shave signs along both roadsides. No doubt reproduced, but wonderful to see nonetheless. A trip back in time for sure!

Peach Springs, Arizona

Peach Springs is located **on US Route 66 that** brought large numbers of cross-country travelers through the town until Interstate 40 was opened 25 miles to the south. The town went from being a popular attraction to being more than thirty miles from the new main highway overnight. The new road shortened the highway distance from Kingman to Seligman by 14 miles at the expense of turning villages like Truxton, Valentine and **Hackberry, Arizona** into ghost towns. Peach Springs survived principally because of the Grand Canyon Caverns located nearby. A similarly named and situated town, Radiator Springs, is depicted in the 2006 **animated** film *Cars* A map with no local off-ramp from I-40 to a largely-parallel US 66 is described in the *Cars* film by town attorney **Sally Carrera** ("the town was bypassed to save ten minutes of driving") leaving vacant, abandoned storefronts after the new road reduced **Main Street** traffic to zero. Similar to Peach Springs, **Route 66** runs on a parallel but less-direct route to the north of I-40.

Figure 47 Peach Springs post card from the Joe Sonderman collection – note the swastikas on building

Figure 48 Peach Springs Trading Post – from the Joe Sonderman post card collection

Grand Canyon Caverns

Located just a few miles east of PeachSprings, Arizona, the caverns lie 230 feet (70 m) below ground level. They are among the largest dry caverns in the United States. Dry caverns compose only 3% of caverns

Figure 49 Caverns entrance

in the world. Because of the lack of water, stalagmites and stalactites are rare in the caverns. Air comes into the caverns from the **Grand Canyon** through 60 miles (97 km) of limestone caves, a fact discovered when red smoke flares were ignited in the caves, and two weeks later, red smoke was seen protruding from vents, near Supai AZ, in the Grand Canyon.

In 1927, cowboy and woodcutter Walter Peck was walking through the area on his way to play poker with his friends when he stumbled and nearly fell into a hole. Peck and some of his friends returned the next day to the large, funnel shaped hole with lanterns and ropes. With a rope tied around his waist, he was lowered into the hole to a depth of 150 feet (46 m), and began exploring.

Speckles on the walls led Peck to think he had discovered a gold mine. He gathered samples of the shiny rocks and had his friends pull him back to the surface. He then purchased the property and began making preparations for a gold mining operation. But once the assay reports were completed, he learned that his potential mother lode was nothing more than iron oxide.

Figure 50 once called Dinosaur Caverns

Today:

The Grand Canyon Caverns are the largest dry caverns in the United States and may be the largest dry cavern system on earth. At a constant 57 °F with only 2 percent humidity year round, the caverns are an ideal preservation area. Cavers and tourists alike can take a 45-minute, guided, walking tour of the caverns beginning with a 21-story, or 210-foot (64 m) descent in an elevator from the surface, or a shorter 25-minute wheelchair-accessible tour.

The Grand Canyon Caverns is a great destination location with an RV park for 800 campers, swimming pool, restaurant and gift shop and market. There is even a 48 room Inn and a 5,000 foot runway for small planes! John McEnulty (owner/partner) extends an invitation to all Route 66 travelers to use their bike and hiking and even horseback riding trails in this beautiful desert area. During the summer months a tour of the caverns will keep you comfortably cool, even *cooler* is the fact you can book a room within the caverns itself!

The Grand Canyon Caverns Inn has a nice RV park and campgrounds. The motel is a great base of operations to explore the Route 66 loop from Kingman to Saligman with fresh air and wide-open spaces. The restaurant has a limited menu – but the food is fresh and well prepared. There is a well stocked convenience store for snacks and staples.

Figure 51 open and airy - a great experience

Figure 52 great food and rooms too!

Figure 53 this is the 'Cave Room' at Grand Canyon Caverns – yes, you can rent it!

I could have spent a week at Grand Canyon Caverns –there's just so much to see and do! They even support several car shows, as one of the owners is a classic car guy himself.

Figure 54 car cruise at Grand Canyon Caverns

CHAPTER
FIVE

Seligman, Arizona

The morning I was leaving Grand Canyon Caverns a staff member pointed out that I had a low right front tire. They had me drive around to the maintenance area, started the air compressor and insisted on filling it for me. (Where do you get service like that?) As the "Caverns" gas station did not have equipment to fix the tire, they suggested that it could be serviced in Seligman-and proceeded to make a call to confirm. (*WHERE DO YOU GET SERVICE LIKE THAT!!*) The staff then gave me complete directions to get there! (WOW!)

Figure 55 their tow and service truck looked a lot like "Mater" from "Cars"

Originally, Seligman was called "Prescott Junction" because it was the railroad stop on the Santa Fe mainline junction with the Prescott and Arizona Central Railway Company feeder line running to Prescott in the Arizona Territory.

Seligman was on the original U.S. Route 66 from 1926 through 1978, when Interstate 40 bypassed it a couple miles south. Seligman experienced its real heyday after World War II, when returning veterans and other motorists hit the road and made the Southwest a popular tourist destination. These days the Seligman Commercial Historic District protects the historical central area's early 20th century commercial buildings along Historic Route 66, a revived popular tourist destination. Contributing properties include: Pitts General Merchandise Store and the U.S. Post Office from 1903, the Pioneer Hall and Theatre and the Seligman Garage from 1905, and the Seligman Pool Hall from 1923.

Figure 56 Angel Delgadillo -'angel' of Seligman

Figure 57 twenty years ago this was a working out-house

In 1987 Seligman gained its name "Birthplace of Historic Route 66" thanks to the efforts of Seligman residents, who convinced the State of Arizona to dedicate Route 66 a historic highway. Seligman is the first stop heading west on the longest uninterrupted stretch of historic Route 66, to Topock, on the east side of the Colorado River. Mr. Angel Delgadillo and his brother Juan own the barber shop and the Snow Cap Ice Cream stand in Seligman and their efforts, are the primary reason Seligman is doing as well as it is! If there was a wigwam motel in this town, this would certainly be "Radiator Springs" from the "Cars" movie.

The growth in Seligman today is mind-blowing compared to five years ago. New businesses thrive, tourists abound and the town itself continues to make improvements. Seligman, Arizona is truly the happy ending as "Radiator Springs" was in the film *Cars.* Both tourists and residents should thank Angel and his brother Juan for the tireless work they invested in bringing a dying town back to being a healthy community.

Figure 58 Sno Cap Ice Cream

Figure 60 Saligman Route 66 Museum

Figure 61 live grazing buffalo

Figure 63 an actual 1860 jail

Figure 62 authentic RR worker's cabin

Figure 65 Seligman garage -20 years ago

Figure 64 Ford truck relic

Figure 66 the one of a kind Snow Cone Chevy

Much has changed in Seligman over the years I've been stopping by – all for the better. People have a renewed interest in the "Old Road" as evidenced by Seligman's success. This road is American history, not just a tired, old highway that has outlived its usefulness in a modern world. Maybe this book will be a call-to-arms for people to stop states like California from closing Route 66 and burying the history of nearly 100 miles of the "Old Road."

The success of Seligman may indirectly help Chambless, Amboy and many other towns and out-of-the-way attractions like the Grand Canyon Caverns and Amboy Crater to name a few.

Figure 67 eating at the "Road Kill Cafe"

Seligman shows that Route 66 still calls to us all –a siren song of the road. More people need to try the best pastrami sandwich at the 'Road Kill Café,' and meet Rudy, who, at Route 66 Automotive, dismantled and repaired my tire – and checked my complete cooling system for $15.00. Route 66: where you can still find iconic Burma Shave signs dotting the roadside. The success of Route 66 is the success of people living in a different America –on Route 66. Meat and potatoes people like the Joad family in *Grapes of Wrath*.

Today it seems, most travelers are destination bound – you see it at crowed airports every day- being jammed into sardine cans with wings; simply wanting the trip to be over. Driving Route 66 *is* the destination you found- the 'Old Road' itself. Smile at the people you meet on Route 66 because they found it too!

Figure 68 a famous Burma Shave sign on '66'

CHAPTER
SIX

ROUTE 66 REVISITED

As a 'car-guy' and writer about classic cars as well as someone who enjoys driving them – especially on Route 66, here are a few photos of my successful and not quite successful Route 66 adventures to show you that I have earned my stripes, to say the least:

1964 – towed my 1960 Jaguar XK-150 from New Jersey to Phoenix, Arizona on the back of a 1962 Chevrolet '409' convertible –(wish I had both of these classics now).

1970 – Moved to California from New Jersey and drove my 1969 special edition Firebird '400'. It broke a fiber timing gear outside of Joplin, Missouri and had to wait three days for parts.

1980 – Attempted to drive my 1950 Ford Coupe on the 'Old Road' but it blew a head-gasket climbing El Cajon Pass (California) in July. I lived in Long Beach, California then.

1983 – Another failed attempt to travel '66' in my 1966 Mercedes 250S but only made it to Gallup, New Mexico. A blizzard had closed all roads to Albuquerque, dropping over a foot of snow and I was reduced to using an ice scraper on the *inside* of my windshield, after both my heater and defroster, not used to such treatment (or use) in southern California, gave-up the ghost.

1990 – Filled with bravado at a local 'cruise-night' at "Johnnie's Drive-In" in Downey, California (where classic cars met on Saturday night) I stated that I would take my 1954 Ford on an 8,000 mile odyssey, driving '66' to Chicago, continuing on to New Jersey for Christmas, down to Florida for the New Year and returning via the southern route. Nobody thought I would be crazy enough to subject my pristine forty-year-old Ford to such winter weather abuse (not to mention myself). The trip was an astounding success! The only problems incurred were a blown seal on my front right wheel (causing it to lock with the lightest touch of the brake pedal)

and a thermostat that was stuck wide-open (forcing me to block part of the radiator to get any heat). My story (and photos documenting the trip) was published in several automotive magazines.

Figure 69 New Jersey snow & ice

Figure 70 Ohio storms

From sunny California. . .

One man's fantasy?

A little 8,000-mile trip from California to New Jersey and back (of course) driving a '54 Ford in winter!

. . .to snowy New Jersey.

I believe that most, if not all, collector car enthusiasts are secret romanticists. They are, additionally, fiercely independent, organized thinkers who, when faced with a challenge, dig right in.

In other words, compared to the rest of today's society, they're considered half crazy.

The following story should remove all doubt about the state of my mental condition. . .I never do things in half measures!

You must know that I am not a native to California (not many are!), but a transplant from another state that has lately been the brunt of off-color humor directed at anyone ever stating that they visited it. I won't name this place for fear of eliciting a similar reaction from you, but it's nestled between New York and Pennsylvania and the initials are N.J.

Now, I'm the kind of guy that enjoys adventure as much as anyone else (have seen all three Indiana Jones movies and I even traveled to Seattle via Amtrack once).

So, when a sunny and warm California November turned into a sunny and warm California December, my thoughts turned to my relatives and friends back east now living in tow-numbing cold in addition to being the objects of "slings and arrows of outrageous humor."

My mistake was reading a book called "Blue Highways" by William Moon, who like myself, found himself without wife or work and decided to follow the siren song of the open road.

"What a novel idea," said one part of my brain to the other. "What an adventure!"

No big deal, I remember thinking to myself. If a guy really wanted to do something special he would strap on, say, a '54 Ford, and do it in the dead of winter. Well, dear reader, I just happen to own a '54 Ford and it was the dead of winter. I was hooked!

The rationalization process was quick, and the momentum of the idea started to build:

Haven't seen the old gang in 20 years, or
Wouldn't it be nice to have a reunion, or
After all, we're not gettin' any younger, and
If we left now, we'd be back there for Christmas!

It's funny the way the mind works. The way my minds works, anyway. For a week the mental battle between the adult and the child raged:

The weather's bad, wait for spring, and
May not have the time in the spring, and
The '54 is old and she may have problems, and
She can do it, and
If I flew, I'd be there in five hours, but that's no fun, and
The old '54 can do it!

I was convinced; the gauntlet was thrown; there was no way out.

60

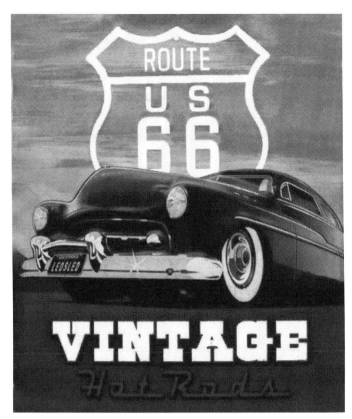

Old Cars & Route 66

The 'Old Road' and old cars go together like ham- on- rye, hand-in-glove or any other metaphor you can think of... it's fun to drive one on the other, even today.

While few of us have the monetary resources of television star Jay Leno to indulge our hobby to extremes as he obviously does, 'car guys' as a rule (now called gear-heads – on the popular English show *Top Gear)* make do with what we have.

I do strongly suggest that, everybody who likes cars, visit the Peterson Auto Museum when in the Los Angeles area-and please bring your lobster bib to keep from drooling on their priceless classics.

Figure 71 Joe Caro's "Bumble Bee"– 1964 Lotus/Westfield Series 3 Super Seven

Derelict cars are like mile markers on Route 66 and in many of the towns along the way. I once found *The Mother Lode* of old cars, in of all places, a used car lot – that hadn't sold a car since 1967!! The car lot is long-gone now, as is its unique owner, but here are a few "treasures" I was able to capture of "Glen's Used Cars."

Figure 72 Glen's Used Cars

Route 66 Pulse

Figure 73 volume 1 issue 1 of the Route 66 Pulse

I like Route 66, I really do. I have driven her narrow roads when she was the "Mother Road" and skirted her pot-holes when she was abandoned by our highway system. When asked to be the editor of a new newspaper called "Route 66 Pulse" several years ago, I jumped at the opportunity. What job, I reasoned, could be a better choice than for someone who loves classic cars *and* classic Route 66 – to write for and manage a newspaper about the "Old Roads "people, places and events. The sad part is "Route 66 Pulse" didn't last but for a few fun and information filled issues.

Working for the "Pulse" was fun, and I really enjoyed my job – especially when I was sent an e-mail from a 10-year-old girl named Mariah Metoyer whom had written a tome about her very first trip aptly named "My Route 66 Trip." Seeing the 'Old Road' viewed through the eyes of this young girl and her family who had never driven Route 66 before, certainly needs mention in this book, as it did in the "Route 66 Pulse "newspaper. While the photo resolution may leave a lot to be desired, her story of " joy and fascination" with the "Grande Dame" of highways holds a special meaning. The words of Tom Snyder (author of the book – *Route 66 Travelers Guide* still ring true: " *. . . you can't keep a good road down. You may take away her destination, even steal her magic numbers but you can't keep old Route 66 out of the hearts and thoughts of three generations of road-borne Americans*".

I awarded Mariah a scale 1962 "Route 66 Pulse" Corvette prize for the fresh excitement and wonder in her words:

Mariah Metoyer and her Mom Karin, winners of the Route 66 Pulse Special Award Corvette for her story "My Route 66 Trip"

My

Route 66 Trip

"Hi, my name is Mariah Metoyer. I am ten years old and going into the 6th. Grade. My dad took me and my sister to see the movie "CARS" It had a lot of stuff about Route 66.

My family and I took a vacation this summer on old Route 66. We started out in Southern California. First we past by the San Andres Fault. I liked it and thought it was pretty cool! After that, we saw a Route 66 sign painted on the road. My mom got out and took some pictures. Then we headed to Amboy and we got off the road and went to Roy's Café. The café was non-operating but there was a man there, and he said that in about a year it would be back in business. He was selling some t-shirts that said Roy's Café Route 66, and I got to buy one.

After we left Roy's we headed to Kingman, Arizona. We had seen these hotels that looked like Tee-Pees called Wig-Wams. I think in the movie it was what the orange cones were. In Kingman we stopped in a place called Quality Inn. They had lots of memorabilia from Route 66.

We drove through this really cool town called Seligman. It had a café there called the Road Kill Café. They had some interesting names for their dishes but the food was awesome! There was an old jail there that we got to walk through. Then back on the road again. We stopped for the night in Flagstaff, Arizona. We ate breakfast and started driving again. We stopped off at the Meteor Crater. The Meteor Crater was a giant hole caused by a huge meteorite that was like. . .

Figure 74 at the "Big Texan"

150 feet across and weighed several hundred thousand tons. We got to look through telescopes to see the other side. It was amazing! We watched a movie and shopped in the gift shop.

On the road again we saw a big billboard sign that said Petrified Forest. The Petrified Forest is made of trees that were buried ages ago and turned to stone by water seeping through the mud and sand into the logs. My dad and I walked through the forest and got to touch a lot of the petrified wood and took pictures while my mom and sister went shopping at the gift shop. We had ice cream there too. The scoops of ice cream there were so big that we asked for half a scoop. Then we drove through the Petrified Forest. It was really cool! We drove into Texas and had a long day so by the time we got there we were pretty tired. We saw a sign for Horse Hotel. I love horses so we had to stay there. It turned out that the Horse Hotel was a hotel for horses but right next to it was the Big Texan so we stayed the night there. The Big Texan was so cool. The comforter was a cow print the doors to go into the bathroom were saloon doors. I thought it was really cool. We got a good night sleep and the next morning we went to have breakfast at the Big Texan restaurant. My sister and I got served our drinks in a boot cup and got to keep them. We had to back track a couple of miles so we could see Arnot Rd. and Cadillac Ranch. Cadillac Ranch was 10 Cadillac's buried half in the ground, half sticking out. They are spray painted a different bunch of colors and people have written things on them. The last thing that we saw on our trip was the leaning water tower. That was my trip on Route 66. I can't wait to do it again!"

Editor's note: Mariah's dad just returned from Iraq and is in the National Guard flying Blackhawk helicopters. This was their first trip to Route 66 From Orange County, California. Originally planning a trip to Missouri to see family and friends when Mariaha and her sister went to see the summer hit "Cars" she asked several times if they could drive part of the way on Route 66. The family enjoyed the trip and they are already planning their next Route 66 outing to the Grand Canyon Caverns in Peach Springs and Oatman, Arizona (Fall, 2006)

CHAPTER
SEVEN

"ROUTE 66"

The TV Show

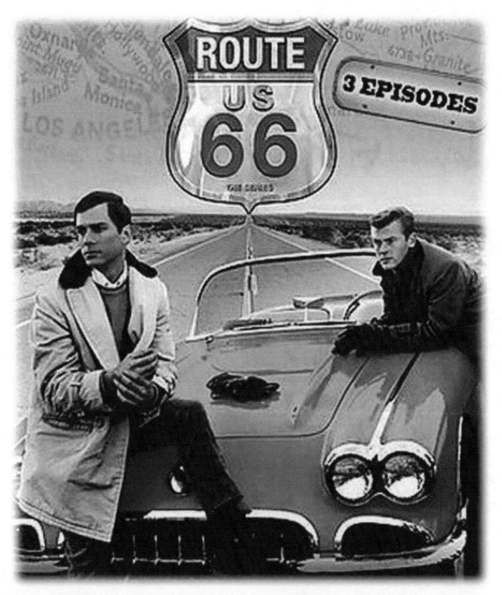

Premiering on CBS television on October 7, 1960 the popular *Route 66* ran for 4 years, starring Martin Milner and George Maharis. When the Milner character, Todd Stiles, is given a new Corvette (and plenty of money) after his father dies, he teams up with his pal from the poor side of town, Buzz Murdock, (George Maharis). After they both decide to leave the cloying expectations of friends and family, for the freedom of open spaces that Route 66 offered, the program takes us from one adventure to the next, a lot like the 1969 *Easy Rider film* with Peter Fonda and Dennis Hopper.

Both Todd and Buzz were, in my opinion, different variants of the Marlon Brando character portrayal in *The Wild One* (1956) with the characters of the TV *Route 66* version substantially more up-market. All three (and even the animated Disney *Cars,*) bring home the fact to the protagonists, that life is about the journey – not the finish line or ending, and that 'living for today' has deeper meanings and responsibilities than the characters ever imagined. The *Route 66* TV show was filmed throughout the U.S. with little filmed on "The Mother Road" itself. The overall theme in this popular program was on the surface "freedom and adventure" as was *Easy Rider* and *The Wild One*. Both freedom and adventure were daily offerings to travelers on Route 66 then . . . and now.

Building Cars for *CARS* the Movie

When John Lasseter was picked to direct the Disney film *Cars* he knew it was the perfect film for him. John had directed his first Disney animated film in 1995 *Toy Story* followed by *A Bugs Life* in 1998 and *Toy Story 2* in 1999. John says of the experience; "I have always loved classic cars. In one vein, I have Disney blood – in the other, there's motor oil! The notion of combining the two great passions of my life was irresistible." When John began filming the movie *Cars,* he knew that he wanted three full-size versions of the main film characters; 'Lightning McQueen' (voiced by Owen Wilson) 'Sally Carrera' (voiced by Bonnie Hunt) and 'Mater' the rascally tow truck (voiced by Larry the Cable Guy). John wanted the cars both for public relations and to promote the film.

Talking about the three cars he wanted with his friend Jay Leno, (The Tonight Show) Jay suggested that he call Eddie Paul at EP Industries in El Segundo, California as the man that can do the job. Not many may recognize his name, but they certainly know his film work: *Grease,* (where Eddie modified 48 cars in two weeks,) *ET* (where Eddie worked on all the special vehicles,) the film *Mask, Dukes of Hazzard, Against All Odds, Cobra, The Fast and the Furious* and many more. They call him "Fast Eddie."

When I asked "Fast Eddie" what he did in his spare time, with a twinkle in his eye he walked me around a partition of his busy shop to a canvass covered hulking shadow, "My latest toy" he exclaimed, and threw the cover off of the biggest, baddest, steroid-induced motorcycle that I've ever seen!

Not only was Eddie's 'toy' powered by a V-8 fuel injected engine, it also carried a supercharger. According to Eddie, this two-wheel monster developed over 1,500 horsepower and weighs a little more than 900 lbs.! In my book, "Fast Eddie" earns his name every time he simply starts this monster up!

Figure 75Eddie Paul (r) working on "Mater's" smile

Fighting a deadline from the very beginning, Eddie and his design and build team worked nearly 24 hours a day knowing that all three vehicles had to be completed before the film premiered. As the due date approached, they actually did work 24 hours a day!

Below are the actual cars built for the film *Cars* that Eddie Paul worked his magic on with the help of his expert building team. "Fast Eddie" just couldn't leave the engines stock in any of these one-of-a-kind vehicles, and while he wouldn't tell me exactly what high-performance additions he made to the *Cars* prototypes, he did start "Lightning McQueen" (the star of the *Cars* film) and rattled windows probably a block away!

The photo on the left shows the soft-spoken Eddie Paul with his patriotic stars and stripes 1,500 horsepower "Boss Hog" which started out as a stock Harley Davidson motorcycle.

Michael Wallis – "Sheriff"

You may remember Michael Wallis's deep, raspy voice as the sheriff in the movie *Cars* but the real Michael Wallis is actually a renowned writer and expert on most all of Route 66, Michael knows every nook and cranny on "The Old Road" much of it explained in his book *Route 66 – The Mother Road*. Michael has been writing since 1968 and became an historian and biographer on the American West, with writings carried by *Time Magazine*, *People Magazine*, the *Smithsonian* and the *New York Times*. Nominated three times for the famed Pulitzer Prize you might think that he is more of a scholar than anything. You would be wrong. The truth is, Michael is just a "regular guy," somebody you would like to have a beer with.

His knowledge of Route 66 is actually how he got the job as the *Cars* sheriff in the first place and is certainly worth repeating:

Hired as an expert on Route 66 by *Cars* director John Lasseter, Michael's job was to take John and his crew on a tour of Route 66 for several weeks, pointing out possible locations for the film. After spending time with Michael and owing to his enthusiasm, humor and distinctive gravelly voice, John offered him the part of "sheriff," then and there. If you would like to find out more about Michael Wallis, you are invited to visit his virtual campfire at: michaelwallis.com.

Drive-In Theatres

On Route 66

Drive-in Daze on Route 66

Pictured: Wayne Simpkins

We can't very well visit "Main Street U.S.A" without a nostalgic look at her past. And a peek at her past wouldn't be complete without the ever-popular drive-in movie theatre would it? Just imagine . . . triple feature films, five cartoons a children's playground, drawings for dinner plates and toasters during intermission plus hot food at the concession stand and fresh popcorn! How can a family evening ever get better than this? People loved outside film viewing so much that in 1947, one entrepreneur built a drive-in fly-in theatre at Monmouth County airport in New Jersey. The cars would park normally with the aircraft parking relegated to an elevated ramp in the back with special speaker stands and access to the active runway.

 Drive-Ins peaked sometime around the early 60s and it's been a downhill tumble ever since. Reportedly in the 1980s over 2,000 drive-ins had closed making room for strip malls and shopping centers. This is directly in-line with the demise of Route 66.

"66" PARK IN THEATRE

LUCINDA LEWIS · ROADSIDE AMERICA

Don't count the drive-in theatres out quite yet however,- there is a resurgence of interest throughout the country by the "baby boomer" generation who fondly recall date nights amorously spent at the local drive-in theatre where "learning french" had little to do with language class at school.

Here are a few drive-in theatres that were on Route 66:

The Purple Passion Drive-In, San Bernardino, CA

The Tee-Pee Drive-In Theatre, Sapula, OK

The Pirate Drive-In, Bristol, OK

The Route 66 Drive-In, (still open) in Springfield, IL

"66" Drive-In theater in Carthage, MO (also open)

Tonto Drive-In, Winslow, AZ

Admiral Twin Drive-In (still open) in Tulsa, OK.

All told, there were around 50 of these wonderful film icons on "The Mother Road" but sadly, almost all are now closed. Or at best, are weekend swap-meet locations or are empty and decaying otherwise.

The few remaining Drive-In theatres on Route 66 are: The Route 66 Drive-In, Springfield, IL, the 19 Drive-In, Cuba, MO, Skyline Drive-In, Barstow, CA, 66 Drive-In, Carthage, MO and the Admiral Drive-In, Tulsa, OK

Little known drive-in facts:

The first actual drive-in theatre opened in New Jersey in 1933, followed years later with a motel drive-in theatre, where you could rent a room and watch the movie from the room's picture window. And yes, the drive-in would accommodate cars as well!

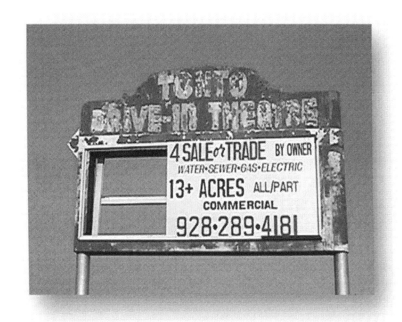

The Drive-In movie was an American lifestyle for over 50 years- the "baby boomer" generation that experienced the *Happy Days* of the 50s, and lived both *American Graffiti and Grease* first- hand as well as Route 66.

I for one, hated to see them all go.

CHAPTER NINE

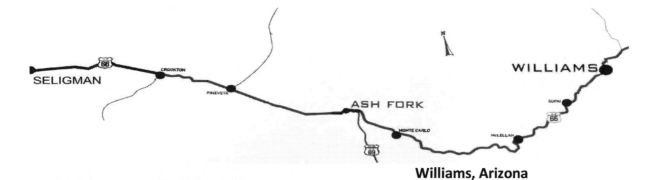

Williams, Arizona

Figure 76 downtown Williams, AZ

Williams was the last town to have its Route 66 highway bypassed, due to lawsuits that kept the last section of Interstate 40 in Arizona from being built around the town. Williams is better known for having several trains that take tourists directly to the Grand Canyon, through a beautiful countryside.

Williams Historic Business District and Urban Route 66, Williams were added to the National Register of Historic Places in 1984 and 1989.

Williams, Arizona is an extraordinary way to enjoy the Grand Canyon. With only an hour travel time to the Grand Canyon- you can stop in Williams for breakfast at a Route 66 corner café, grab your souvenirs, hop on a train, visit a wildlife park, take a hike, grab a pole and head out fishing, or simply stroll the streets before your drive to the Canyon on highway 64.

Figure 77 steam train to Grand Canyon

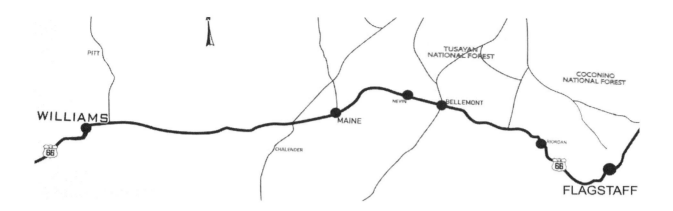

Grand Canyon, Arizona

Unique combinations of geologic color and erosion decorate a canyon that is 277 river miles (446km) long, up to 18 miles (29km) wide, and a mile (1.6km) deep. Grand Canyon overwhelms your senses through its immense size.

The road to the Grand Canyon from the south (Highway 180 out of Flagstaff) crosses a gently rising plateau that gives no hint at what is about to unfold. You wonder if you have made a wrong turn. All at once an immense gorge a mile deep and up to 18 miles wide opens up. The scale is so vast that even from the best vantage point only a fraction of the canyon's 277 miles can be seen.

Nearly five million people travel to the Grand Canyon each year; 90 percent first see the canyon from the South Rim with its dramatic views into the deep inner gorge of the Colorado River. So many feet have stepped cautiously to the edge of major overlooks that in places the rock has been polished smooth. But most of the park's 1,904 square miles are maintained as wilderness. You can avoid crowds by hiking the park's many trails or driving to the cool evergreen forests of the North Rim where people are fewer and viewing is more leisurely.

The Grand Canyon boasts some of the nation's cleanest air, with visibility on clear days averaging 90 to 110 miles.

A great drive to the Canyon—a spectacular sight when you get there.

Flagstaff, Arizona

Flagstaff's early economy was based on the lumber, railroad, and ranching industries. Today, the city remains an important distribution hub for companies such as Nestlé Purina PetCare, and is home to Lowell Observatory The U.S. Naval Observatory, the United States Geological Survey Flagstaff Station, and Northern Arizona University. Flagstaff has a strong tourism sector, due to its proximity to Grand Canyon National Park, Oak Creek Canyon, the Arizona the Snowbowl, Meteor Crater, and historic Route 66 which is now I-40 (also called Purple Heart Trail.

Figure   78 old Route 66 out of Flagstaff is now I-40

If you can, spend some time just driving around in this beautiful countryside –take a trip to Oak Creek Canyon (I-17 south also called Black Canyon Freeway) which will take you all the way to Phoenix, Arizona.

During a 1950s Trailways bus trip (remember Trailways?)   from Phoenix to New Jersey in the middle of winter, the bus drove up to Flagstaff through Oak Creek Canyon, in snow, at night. It was certainly an adventure! When arriving at the Flagstaff bus terminal in the early morning hours, I found that snow and Ice had closed Route 66 in both directions. I was stranded in Flagstaff for two beautiful days!

You may enjoy a drive to the Sedona area – the most beautiful country you will find. Highway 89A south will get you there from Flagstaff.

The destination for all seasons, Flagstaff is alive with cultural diversity, beauty, history and recreational and scientific opportunities. At a cool 7,000-foot elevation, located in the world's largest ponderosa pine forest, Flagstaff is near seven national parks and monuments and 80 miles from the Grand Canyon. Northern Arizona is also rich in Native American history and culture with nearby Navajo and Hopi reservations.

A phantom bell boy, murdered prostitutes, and a booze-loving criminal are just a few of the ghosts said to haunt the Hotel Monte Vista in Flagstaff, AZ. In fact, John Wayne himself, encountered a spirit at the 87-year-old landmark. There is a macabre story behind the hotels infamous hauntings.

Figure 79 the haunted Hotel Monte Vista

CHAPTER TEN

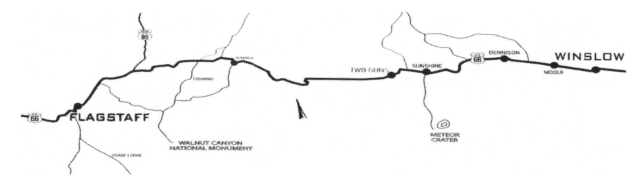

Meteor Crater

Driving east out of Flagstaff you will enjoy beautiful desert countryside and clean air on I-40 which mostly has overlapped Route 66. Your suggested destination, several miles ahead, is the famous Meteor Crater. While not nearly as impressive as the Grand Canyon, nor as deep, Meteor Crater, as the

Figure 81 road to Meteor Crater-you can see crater edges in the distance

name implies, is exactly that. This huge depression, 0.74 miles in diameter and 550 feet deep was created 49,000 years ago by meteoric impact, and its proximity to the interstate now attracts many visitors despite the high cost of entry – the crater has been privately owned by the same family since early investigations began in 1902 by Daniel M. Barringer, and is now a thriving commercial enterprise complete with such modern requirements as a movie theater, restaurant and gift shop. Entry prices (2014) are $16 per adult or $8 per child (free for the under five). Crater road as you can see from the above map – is a six-mile drive once you exit Route 66 to the south.

Figure 80 amazing Meteor Crater

This aerial photo gives you a full perspective of the actual size of Meteor Crater. The access road is that thin ribbon of black on the right side.

Winslow, Arizona

Route 66 was routed through downtown Winslow, Arizona. A contract to build Interstate 40 as a bypass north of Winslow was awarded at the end of 1977. A small town of about 6,000 people Winslow is the home of the last Harvey House built (La Posada Hotel) which opened in 1930. It was designed by Mary Colter The hotel closed in 1957 and was used by the Santa Fe Railway for offices. The railroad abandoned La Posada in 1994 and announced plans to tear it down. It was saved by Route 66 fans, and it currently serves as a hotel once again.

Winslow achieved national fame in 1972 in the Eagles / Jackson Browne song "Take it Easy" which contains the lyrics –*standin' on a corner in Winslow, Arizona.*

There's a magic about the city of Winslow. Take just a moment to stop and look around, and you'll discover a whole new dimension to this unique western city (states the Chamber of Commerce).

Civilizations have thrived in the area for centuries the ancient Hopi village of Homolovi, the Mormon settlement of Brigham City, the booming town of Winslow over 100 years ago.

More recent additions to the City of Winslow are The "Standin' on the Corner Park," which has become an interesting draw for music fans who remember the line –*standin' on the corner in Winslow Arizona, such a fine sight to see,* from the #1 hit *Take It Easy,* sung by the Eagles.

Holbrook, Arizona

A few miles east of Winslow on Route 66 you will find Holbrook, Arizona. Holbrook began as a railroad stop in 1881 and is a small rural town on Route 66 In 1912 a meteorite exploded over town showering Holbrook with fragments. Known as the Holbrook Meteorite, many fragments have been collected and are on display today. Holbrook is 28 miles

west of the Petrified Forest National Park, and the home of the "Wigwam Motel" built in 1950 and related to the San Bernardino, California cousin with the same name.

When I stayed at the Wigwam Motel I noticed the remains of a 1936 Ford by a fence in the parking lot. When I asked the staff I was told a remarkable story about a family that arrived in the 50s and stayed at the Wigwam but couldn't pay their bill. They left the car for security saying they would return. The car still sits where they parked it – over 50 years ago.

While I took this photo several years ago, I have the feeling that the Ford is still there.

Petrified Forest – Painted Desert, Arizona

The Painted Desert encompasses over 93,500 acres and stretches over 160 miles. It begins about 30 miles north of Cameron, Arizona near the southeastern rim of the Grand Canyon to the Petrified Forest about 26 miles east of Holbrook, AZ. Along the way, it grazes the backyard of the Wupatki National Monument Indian Ruins. The Painted Desert derives its name for the multitude of colors ranging from lavenders to shades of gray with vibrant colors of red, orange and pink. It is a long expanse of badland hills and buttes and although barren and austere, it is a beautiful landscape of a rainbow of colors. As you drive old Route 66 you will also notice unusual outcroppings which are petrified pine trees. The handiwork of erosion, water, and silica, the remnants of this once magnificent pine forest have taken millions of years to resurface, and sparkle like so many diamonds. Once the stomping ground of dinosaurs and other prehistoric residents, the Petrified Forest continually reveals the skeletons of its stormy past

Take the Park Road exit off Route 66 to get to the park museum and a short drive through the Petrified Forest itself. Bring your camera.

The Petrified Forest is known for its fossils, especially fallen trees that lived in the Late Triassic about 225 million years ago. The sediments containing the fossil logs are part of the widespread and colorful Chinle Formation from which the Painted Desert gets its name.

In Petrified Forest National Park, most of the logs in the park retained their original external form during petrification but lost their internal structure. However, a small fraction of the logs and most of the park's petrified animal bones have cells and other spaces that are mineral-filled but still retain much of their original organic structure.

No, you can't take any samples home with you. Park Rangers frown on that!

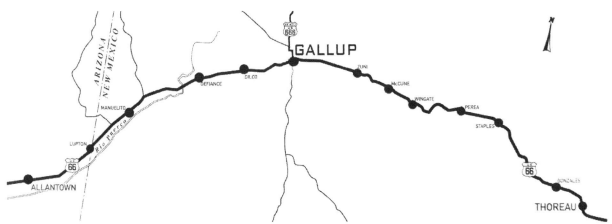

Crossing the Arizona/New Mexico border on the 'Old Road' will bring you to the Famous TeePee Trading Post, Lupton, AZ.

Figure 83TeePee Trading Post

Figure 82 my 250S Mercedes makes it to Lupton

Commercial tourist "TeePee's" where used extensively throughout Indian country from Arizona to Missouri (with the exception of the Wigwam Motel in San Bernardino, CA) To give you some idea of when these photos were taken, notice the cigarette ad prices of $7.99 a carton! I believe it's around $50. today.

Driving on Route 66 is not without drawbacks – you may come to the end of the road –like the photo of the Mercedes, and have to back-track miles to regain I-40.

Gallup, New Mexico

U.S. Route 66 passes through Gallup, and the town's name is mentioned in the lyrics of the song *Get Your Kicks on Route 66*. In 2003, the U.S. and New Mexico Departments of Transportation renumbered US Highway 666, the city's other major highway, (see chapter two –Mysteries & Ghosts) as Route 491. Former Governor Bill Richardson pushed for (and got) the number changed because "666" is associated with Satan and Devil worship, and thus it was considered "cursed" or a "Beast" to some locals. The situation was exacerbated by the high death toll on the highway, which was largely attributed to high rates of drivers under the influence of alcohol or drugs

Figure 84 night photo by Ricgie Diesterheft

Hollywood, New Mexico –The Gallup El Rancho Hotel was built in 1936 along U.S. Route 66 for Mr. R.E. "Griff" Griffith, brother of the famous movie director D.W. Griffith. El Rancho Hotel is a large, rambling, rustic style building that still feeds the fantasy of the Old West in Gallup, New Mexico. The El Rancho continued to be linked to Hollywood and the movie industry until the mid-1960s. Ronald Reagan, John Wayne, Katherine Hepburn, Spencer Tracy, Errol Flynn, Kirk Douglas, Gregory Peck, and Humphrey Bogart are only a few of the film stars who stayed at the hotel while making movies in the vicinity

Both Griff and his brother encouraged moviemakers to use El Rancho as a base for crews and stars on location because of its proximity to striking western landscapes and the hotel's rustic elegance. When it opened in 1936, the El Rancho boasted superior service and accommodations for roughing it in comfort.

Figure 85 I took this photo of the Log Cabins in 1989

Located on Route 66 west of Gallup, the Log Cabin Lodge has eked-out a poor existence for many years and I am told is abandoned and in poor repair from its heyday in the 1940s.

Figure 86 post card of the Log Cabin Lodge -1940s

In the late 80s I became stranded in Gallup for three days. Driving my Mercedes 250S on Route 66 in the middle of winter, what was a mild snow storm in Gallup was a blizzard at my next port-of-call, Albuquerque. I-40 (Route 66) was closed to all traffic going up the grade, with more snow expected. With a non-functioning heater and defroster in the 1966 Mercedes, I limped back to Gallup in time to get the last possible room in town. If I would have gone to the nearby train station and slept on a cold, hard, drafty bench, and eaten stale vend-o sandwiches, I would have been much happier!

CHAPTER
ELEVEN

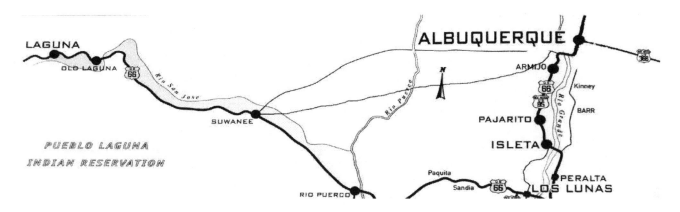

You will have about a 140 mile drive between Gallup and Albuquerque, New Mexico to enjoy the scenic beauty of the countryside. For the most part, I-40 overlaps Route 66 all the way to Mesita, then short-cuts across to Albuquerque, while Route 66 first goes to Los Lunas before it turns left to enter the city.

Outside of a few rusted hulks of Fords and Chevy's along the way, the beauty of the New

Mexico desert will be unimpaired. There is a mining museum to see in Grants, NM on Route 66.

Figure 87 Grants mining museum

Albuquerque, New Mexico

The first travelers on Route 66 appeared in Albuquerque in 1926, and before long, dozens of motels, restaurants, and gift shops had sprung up along the roadside to serve them. Route 66 originally ran through this nearly mile-high city on a north-south alignment along Fourth Street, but in 1937 it was realigned along Central Avenue a more direct east-west route. The intersection of Fourth and Central downtown was the principal crossroads of the city for decades. The majority of the surviving structures from the Route 66 era are on Central, though there are also some on Fourth. Signs between Bernalillo and Los Lunas along the old route now have brown, historical highway markers denoting it as *Pre-1937 Route 66.*

Figure 88 hot air balloons dot the Albuquerque sky

With over a half- million people, Albuquerque has all of the advantages of a large city, but has lost the charm that Route 66 once brought here. The first week in October the city sponsors the Albuquerque International Balloon Festival filled with events, music and food. If this is your thing, call ahead for your room. This high desert city has an altitude approaching 5,000' and, as I found out on several winter '66' trips, has more than its share of snow and storms. While I-40 leaves the city to the east, Route 66 (Highway 25) rambles north to Santa Fe and Pecos, New Mexico, rejoining I-40 at Santa Rosa.

Santa Rosa, New Mexico

Santa Rosa's stretch of U.S. Route 66 is part of film history. When John Steinbeck's epic novel, *The Grapes of Wrath*, was made into a movie, director John Ford used Santa Rosa for the memorable train scene. Tom Joad (Henry Fonda) watches a freight train steam over the Pecos River railroad bridge, into the sunset. It was also one of shooting scenes for *Bobbie Jo and the Outlaw* starring Lynda Carter in the title role.

Santa Rosa, owes a large part of its designation as "The Scuba Diving Capital of the Southwest" to the "Blue Hole," a 81-foot-deep natural artesian spring that—at 62 degrees—allows for year-round scuba diving. In warmer months you can relax with a dip and experience the joys of swimming 'al fresco' in the natural spots and deep swimming holes in Santa Rosa.

To me, the best part of this wonderful little town is the Route 66 Auto Museum. This, you just can't miss!

Figure 89 got to see I Route 66 Auto Museum!

Just off of I-40 on historic US-66 east of downtown Santa Rosa is the Route 66 Auto Museum, owned by Santa Rosa local mechanic and hot-rodder James "Bozo" Cordova. Featuring a modest yet excellent collection of original vintage, classic, and hot-rod automobiles and trucks, the small museum is a slice of a classic Route 66 town in its heyday. Featuring cars, signage, and all types of classic and hot-rod memorabilia, visitors are greeted by friendly staff. The price of admission is $5 a person, but there are plenty vehicles to look at for free outside. The museum alone is worth the stop, but the town is pleasant and the drive full of excellent scenery, a perfect place for gas and a break to soak in some local culture.

Tucumcari, New Mexico

Fifty miles east of Santa Rosa on Route 66 (I-40) will bring you to Tucumcari, New Mexico. Originally called Ragtown, in 1901, the camp became known as "Six Shooter Siding", due to numerous gunfights. Its first formal name, Douglas, was used only for a short time. After it grew into a permanent settlement, it was renamed Tucumcari in 1908. The name was taken from Tucumcari Mountain which is situated near the community.

Old U.S. Route 66 runs through the heart of Tucumcari via Route 66 Boulevard, which was previously known as Tucumcari Boulevard from 1970 to 2003 and as Gaynell Avenue before that time. Numerous businesses, including gasoline service stations, restaurants and motels, were constructed to accommodate tourists as they traveled through on the 'Mother Road.' A large number of the vintage motels and restaurants built in the 1930s, 1940s, and 1950s are still in business despite intense competition from newer chain motels and restaurants in the vicinity of Interstate 40, which passes through the city's outskirts on the south.

Figure 90 Blue Swallow Motel

Tucumcari, New Mexico recognizes and honors its relationship with Route 66. Many of the eateries and motels have been carefully restored to the 1950s look that made them popular for tourists and travelers back then. There is much Route 66 nostalgia in this little town that grew and prospered during the Route 66 era. The town is almost a time-warp back to the 50s! Route 66 runs through the center of town. Today, with a population of over 6,000, Tucumcari provides a number of area attractions including The Mesa Lands Dinosaur Museum, The Tucumcari Historical Museum which includes a historic Route 66 exhibit, and Ute Lake State Park

FIGURE 91   A LOCAL POPULAR TUCUMCARI EATERY ON ROUTE 66

FIGURE 92   TUCUMCARI MONUMENT TO ROUTE 66

7

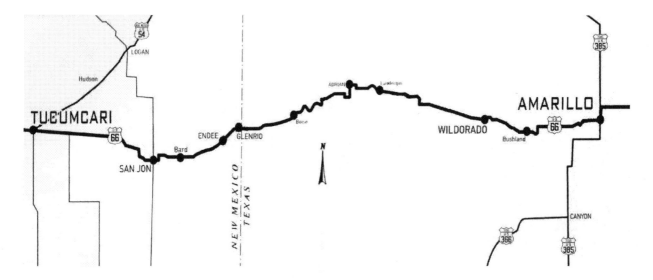

Cadillac Ranch

Nine miles west of Amarillo is the famous 'Cadillac Ranch' which is a necessary stop for the curious and those wishing to pay indirect tribute to how cars in general, changed many lives as they traveled Route 66.

Standing along Route 66 west of Amarillo, Texas, 'Cadillac Ranch' was invented and built by a group of art-hippies imported from San Francisco. They called themselves The Ant Farm, and their silent partner was Amarillo billionaire Stanley Marsh. Marsh wanted a piece of public art that would baffle the locals, and the hippies came up with a tribute to the evolution of the Cadillac tail fin. Ten Caddies were driven into one of Stanley Marsh's fields, then half-buried, nose-down, in the dirt (supposedly at the same angle as the Great Pyramid of Giza). They faced west in a line, from the 1949 Club Sedan to the 1963 Sedan de Ville, their tail fins held high for all to see on the empty Texas panhandle.

Figure 93 Cadillac Ranch photo art by James Kalimino

CHAPTER
TWELVE

"The Big Texan" is a must (even if you don't relish steaks) is located a few miles from Cadillac Ranch. This iconic steak house (home of the famous free 72 oz. steak) opened in 1960 on old '66' and is now located off exit 74 off I-40. A favorite stop for ten-year-old Mariah Metoyer (See her story in an earlier chapter) "The Big Texan" and its "Big Cowboy" statue is a favorite stop for Route 66 travelers as well.

This is the perfectly grilled 72 oz. steak that is absolutely *FREE* if you can eat it in an hour. "The Big Texan" has a full menu for everyone – but is a steak eater's dream! Have fun here and "*mangia-mangia*" as my sainted Italian grandmother would say.

Amarillo, Texas

Amarillo, Texas was hit by the Dust Bowl in the 1930S and entered an economic depression. It counted on U.S. Routes 60, 87, 287, and 66 that merged at Amarillo, making it a major tourist stop with numerous motels, restaurants, and staples for travelers back then, heading to California. With over 130,000 residents this town is much more contemporary urban than most towns its size. Not much left of Route 66 to explore.

Figure 94 the Big Boot –at the Big Texan Steak House

Groom, Texas

There are only about 500 residents in Groom, Texas spread-out in this agricultural area. The most interesting attraction on Route 66, in my opinion, is a 19-story cross located next to Interstate 40 just northwest of the town limits. This 190-foot-tall (58 m) free-standing cross can be seen from 20 miles (32 km) away. Surrounding the base of the cross are life-sized statues of the 14 Stations of the Cross. There is an authentic copy of the Shroud of Turin there as well as meditation areas and pools. Admission is free but you can leave a contribution. After eating my fill at "The Big Texan" Steak House and before hitting the highway –I often spend an hour or two at "The Cross" if for no other reason, but to rest up enough to continue my journey.

You must ask yourself why the water tower is in this location in the first place? Many think it was built just like it is simply for attention. Not so, "The Route 66 Cross."

Figure 95 the leaning tower of Groom

Figure 96 "The Cross of Route 66"

There is quite a story about what I call "The Route 66 Cross" but I am not going to ruin it for you by disclosing it in this book. I will say that it was built by a man who promised to share the blessings the Lord gave him. Sitting in what was once a cotton field, the many acres of this retreat were donated by a farmer who was himself, spiritually helped. You may scoff at this Marine Corps veteran for becoming maudlin, but this is a very special area indeed!

If you drive around the area a bit, you will locate the remains of the town of Groom, Texas as well as a few abandoned houses that were directly on "The Old Road."

Our next stop of interest is Shamrock, Texas and the Tower Service Station that resolved our overheating problem in the summer of 1956.

Figure 97 the restored Tower Station

Shamrock, Texas

This town of 2,000 residents was well located on old Route 66 as an oasis in the desert and had a full service at the Tower Station and the best food in the panhandle at the "U Drop In" attached café. A magnet on Route 66 since 1936, the Tower Station has been restored as a visitor's center.

Figure 98 remnants of a old '66' gift shop

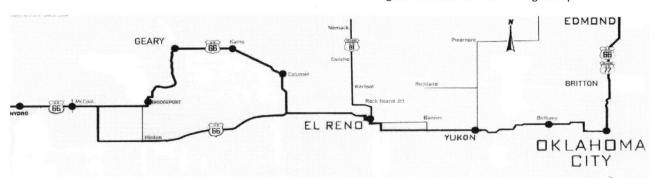

Oklahoma City, Oklahoma

Oklahoma City was a major stop on Route 66 during the early part of the 20th century; it was prominently mentioned in Bobby Troup's 1946 jazz classic, "(Get Your Kicks on) Route 66", later made famous by artist Nat King Cole. A city of over a million residents, while *Oklahoma City is mighty pretty* in the Bobby Troup song – there is very little that remains an attraction to Route 66 travelers. If you swing north on Highway 35 and follow '66' you will come to Arcadia, Oklahoma, which has: the world's largest soda bottle (with straw) a wonderful Route 66 Museum and the famous "Round Barn of Arcadia."

Figure 99 65' soda bottle at "Pop's"

Arcadia, Oklahoma is actually suburb of Oklahoma City, and has about 200 residents living there. Its home is on Route 66 and it has several remarkable items of interest for the traveler. "Pop's" is known as the soda (soft drink) capitol carrying over 700 brands of your favorite soft-drink (including Route 66 soda).

Sitting atop a low terrace overlooking the Deep Fork River, the Round Barn in Arcadia has been a center of community activity and curiosity for over a century. William Harrison "Big Bill" Odor arrived in Oklahoma County in 1892, and shortly after, in 1898, oxen cleared the ground for construction of

his barn. He built a barn 60 feet in diameter and 43 feet high with a local red Permian rock foundation. Local burr oak timbers were soaked in water until soft and then banded into the mold to create the rafters. Mr. Odor apparently designed the barn himself, though no one knows how he chose the round design. Only partially standing in the 1970s, the Arcadia Historical Society spent several years restoring it to original condition.

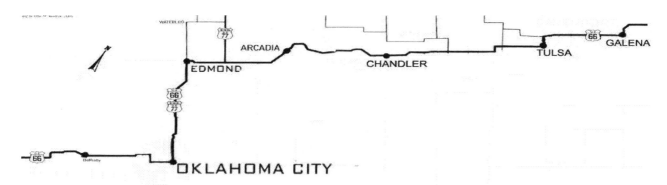

Not much is happening as far as sightseeing 'till you reach Catoosa, (which is not shown on map,) but is a few miles east of Tulsa, Oklahoma on Route 66. And a half-mile east of Catoosa on Route 66 is the "Blue Whale" which once was a swim park on '66' and is now a picnic area.

Built in 1972 as an anniversary gift, the Blue Whale quickly evolved into a local summer hot spot and family travel destination. Almost immediately the whale began attracting people who wanted to fling

themselves off his tail, slide down his water-coated fins and poke their heads out the holes in the whale's head. Travelers stopped by to picnic, swim, or fish. So began what became one of the best loved icons on Route 66.

Thirty miles further up Route 66 to the town of Afton you will find the car museum Afton Station (12 SE First Street) that has a display of old Packard's for you to see and a gift shop.

While you are driving in this area you may wish to head a little further north on Old '66' a mile past Narcissa (also not on the map) so you can drive the "Ribbon Highway" which is a 9' wide original Route 66 roadway, (which is hopefully better than the Newbery Springs stretch of road in California.)

Driving a little further to Galena (this *is* on the map) is your last stop in Oklahoma to see "Cars on the Route" which is a restored 30s gas station painstakingly restored to original condition (119 N. Main Street).

Interstate I-40 is now Interstate I-44 in Missouri, overlapping Route 66.

CHAPTER
THIRTEEN

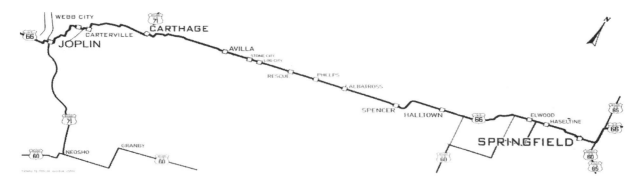

Figure 100 one of the few remaining Drive-Ins on Route 66

Joplin, Missouri

While Joplin was first settled for lead mining, zinc, often referred to as "jack," was the most important mineral resource. As railroads were built to connect Joplin to major markets in other cities, it was on the verge of dramatic growth. By the start of the 20th Century, the city was becoming a regional metropolis. Construction centered around Main Street, with many bars, hotels, and fine homes nearby.

Joplin's three-story "House of Lords" was its most famous saloon, with a bar and restaurant on the first floor, gambling on the second and a brothel on the third. Trolley and rail lines made Joplin the hub of southwest Missouri. As the center of the "Tri-state district", it soon became the lead and zinc mining capital of the world.

There is not much left of Route 66 to interest travelers –with the exception of the Route 66 Drive-In theatre (closed from mid-September to April).

First opened in 1949 the "66 Drive-In" closed in the mid-70S – was totally restored and now provides Friday –Sunday feature films from the Spring to Fall months.

Springfield, Missouri

Recognized by convention as the "Birthplace of US Route 66", it was in Springfield on April 30, 1926 that officials first proposed the name of the new Chicago-to-Los Angeles highway.

John T. Woodruff of Springfield was elected as the first president of the U.S. Highway 66 Association, organized in Tulsa, Oklahoma in 1927. Its purpose was to get U.S. 66 paved from end- to- end and to promote tourism on the highway. In 1938, Route 66 became the first completely paved numbered highway in America — "Main Street America" — stretching from the Great Lakes to the Pacific Coast.

Figure 101 Reds Giant Hamburg art by Phil Jackson

A placard in Park Central Square was dedicated to the city by the Route 66 Association of Missouri, and traces of the Mother Road are still visible in Downtown Springfield along Kearney Street, Glenstone Avenue, College and St. Louis streets and on Missouri 266 to Halltown. The red booths and gleaming chrome in mom-and-pop diners, the stone cottages of tourist courts and the many service stations along this route saw America fall in love with the automobile.

Red's Giant Hamburg, is said to be the birthplace of the drive-up order window, and was located on the route. Red and Julia Chaney opened America's first drive-through hamburger joint in 1947 after Red learned "fast food" had a future while working for the Heinz Company. The Giant Hamburg on West Chestnut Expressway was a Route 66 mainstay until it closed for good in December 1984. When Mr. and Mrs. Chaney retired in 1984, customers stood for hours in a long line weaving down the old Route 66 roadway. The restaurant's food supply was empty by mid-afternoon and the doors were locked with the final crowd inside to share their last fun meal / visit with the twosome and try to memorialize the historic ending.

Figure 102 even though the business is gone, the sign has been reproduced
in memory of the much loved drive-thru.

St. Robert, Missouri

There is much of Route 66 left between Springfield and St. Louis; you just have to explore to sometimes find it. A good example is the town of St. Robert –The major east-west route is Interstate 44; before that, the main highway was U.S. Route 66, which still exists as a scenic route through the area and passes through Devil's Elbow, St. Robert, Waynesville, Buckhorn and Hazelgreen. Names for U.S. Route 66 vary – at different places; it's called Teardrop Road, Highway Z, Old Route 66, Historic Route 66, and Highway 17. State-posted signs mark most of the alignment of the road.

Cuba, Missouri –"Route 66 Mural City"

Cuba was designated as the Route 66 Mural City by the Missouri legislature in recognition of Viva Cuba's Outdoor Mural Project. The beautification group consulted with Michelle Loughery, a Canadian muralist who helped create a vision and two of the murals. The group commissioned twelve outdoor murals along the Route 66 corridor. Interstate 44 now runs through Cuba. The Wagon Wheel Motel is a historic landmark and has been a presence on Route 66 since the 1930s. The guest cottages and old Wagon Wheel building underwent renovations beginning in 2009.

Figure 103 two of the many beautiful building murals in Cuba, Missouri

Meramec Caverns

A few miles before you enter Stanton, Missouri on I-44 you will see signs for the Meramec Caverns which is the largest commercial cave in the state of Missouri. Missouri is also known as the Cave State, hosting home to more than 6,000 surveyed caves. Meramec Caverns is open year round and offers a fun, affordable vacation for all its visitors. The caverns were formed from the erosion of large **limestone** deposits over millions of years. **Pre-Columbian Native American** artifacts have been found in the caverns. Currently the cavern system is a **tourist attraction**, with more than fifty billboards along **Interstate 44** and is considered one of the primary attractions along former **Highway 66**.

St. Louis, Missouri

St. Louis is the largest city along Route 66 between Chicago and Los Angeles, and there are a number of sites related to the 'Mother Road' within the region. Some of the streets have new names, but all of these locations are part of the Route 66 journey including the famous St. Louis Arch and the Route 66 Chain of Rocks Bridge just to name a couple. An iconic Route 66

attraction that's been around since 1941 is Ted Drewes Frozen Custard stand (6726 Chippewa Street). The specialty here is concrete – edible, of course. Concretes are über-thick milkshakes made from vanilla frozen custard and blended with any number of sweet treats. Try the 'Cardinal Sin' (hot fudge and tart cherries), get 'All Shook Up' (peanut butter and bananas) or make up your own creation.

For you 'car guys' there is something special – go to the St. Louis Museum of Transportation and check-out the late singer Bobby Darin's one-of-a-kind car! Designed by Andrew Di Dia (the famous clothes designer in 1961). Called the "Di Dia 150" it cost over $90,000 to build in 1960 dollars.

I won't spoil it for you with all the details, but this one attraction may make your entire trip!
I will say that Darin took his wife Sandra Dee, to the Academy Awards in it in 1961.

Figure 104 singer Bobby Darin and his "Di Dia 150"

Figure 105 St. Louis 'Gateway' arch

The **Gateway Arch** is a 630-foot (192 m) monument in St. Louis in the U.S. state of Missouri. Clad in stainless steel and built in the form of an inverted, weighted catenary arch, it is the world's tallest arch, the tallest monument in the Hemisphere, and Missouri's tallest accessible building. Built as a monument to the westward expansion of the United States it is the centerpiece of the Jefferson National Expansion Memorial and has become an internationally famous symbol of St. Louis.

Chain of Rocks Bridge

Chain of Rocks Bridge is one of the more interesting bridges in America. It's hard to forget a 30-degree turn midway across a mile-long bridge more than 60 feet above the mighty Mississippi. For more than three decades, the bridge was a significant landmark for travelers driving Route 66.

The bridge's colorful name came from a 17-mile shoal, or series of rocky rapids, called the Chain of Rocks beginning just north of St. Louis. Multiple rock ledges just under the surface made this stretch of the Mississippi River extremely dangerous to navigate. Located three miles west of Granite City, this was the only crossing point on Route 66 of the Mississippi River. Opened in 1929, the bridge is no longer open to auto traffic but is a bike trail linking scenic areas on both sides of the river.

Figure 106 Chain of Rocks bridge makes a 30 degree turn mid-stream

Figure 107 travelers rest on Route 66 bench

CHAPTER FOURTEEN

Soulsby Station

Leaving St. Louis on I-55 (overlaps Route 66) you could stop in Hamel at "Weezy's Route 66 Bar & Grill" (off at exit 30 to 108 Old Route 66) this little café has been serving travelers since the 1940s and is truly an early diner.

A few miles further will take you to Mt. Olive, where you will find Soulsby Service Station – (exit 44 to Old Route 66 – if you're not already on it). This station was opened in 1926 and is a perfect example of the old "house and canopy" style popular back then.

Figure 108 the original Soulsby Station

The image on the right is the restored Soulsby Service Station which looks pretty authentic, all things considered. The station is no longer open for business but it is certainly something nice to see in a preserved condition.

Springfield, Illinois

The spirit of the "Land of Lincoln" is nowhere else so alive as it is in Springfield, one time home to old 'Honest Abe' himself and present home of the Lincoln Home National Historic Site, the Lincoln-Herndon Law Offices State Historic Site, the Old State Capitol State Historic Site, the Abraham Lincoln Presidential Library and Museum and the Lincoln Tomb State Historic Site. Almost as important – Springfield is the home of the "Cozy Dog" (2935 S. 6th. Street – which is business 55 and historic 66). This is the home of the first 'hot- dog- on- a –stick' invented back in 1940. Still owned by the same family, this popular eatery offered, then and now, 'Cozy Dogs' to travelers on Route 66. You can watch the staff actually make your 'Cozy Dogs' as long as you don't call them – hot dogs on a stick or worse, corn dogs!

The **Cozy Dog Drive In** is a restaurant located at 2935 South Sixth Street in Springfield, Illinois which claims to be the first place to serve the corn dog. The claim states that the deep fried, battered hot dog on a stick was invented by Ed Waldmire Jr. and his friend, Don Strand while they were stationed at an Amarillo, Texas base in World War II. However, others also claim to have invented it earlier, such as Pronto Pup vendors at the Minnesota State Fair but I believe it was served here first.

Figure 109 'dog on a stick on 66'

Figure 111 happy Cozy Dog customer holding my

Route '66' art

Figure 110 the Cozy Dog icons

Figure 112 making the famous Cozy Dog

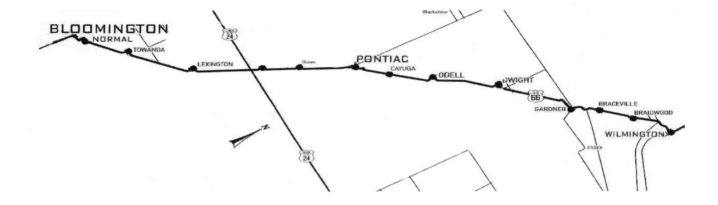

Henry's Rabbit Ranch, Staunton, Illinois

Away from the maddening crowds, on old Route 66 (I-55 exit 41. Drive west on Staunton Rd. Take the third left onto Old Route 66 and follow it southwest. Rabbit Ranch will be on the right, just before Madison St. Look for the semi trailers parked in front).

With its front yard on Route 66, Henry's Rabbit Ranch hops over countless other self-referential Mother Road attractions with its population of live bunnies. Owner and chief rabbit wrangler Rich Henry is outnumbered by a fuzzy populace that peaked at around 50 in 2003 (a love explosion) then gradually diminished to a more manageable 20 through careful neutering. "Back then people were saying, 'You oughta go for 66!" said Rich. "I couldn't handle that."

Figure 113 Henry's Route 66 sign

Figure 114 Rich Henry feeding 'Bugs'

I have no idea how I found Rich Henry's place – I must have gotten lost at some point. A nicer guy with very extensive knowledge of Route 66 would be hard to find. He's more than happy to tell you stories (he *likes* stories), show you around his rabbits and his very nifty store and shop. Anyone that puts a Route 66 decal on his motorcycle tank can't be all bad!

Figure 115 Henry's Rabbit Ranch store front

Odell, Illinois

In 1921 the state put under contract a highway paving project for what at first was known as the *Chicago-Springfield East St. Louis Road*. Paving was finished through Odell in 1922. The designation of the road was soon changed to Route 4. In 1926, what was substantially the same road became **Route 66**. At first all of these roads passed through the center of Odell and by 1933 the local citizens became so frustrated by the inability of people to cross the road that they constructed a pedestrian underpass beneath the highway.

Figure 116 Standard Oil station in Odell, Illinois

A Standard Oil sign hanging from the roof swings gently in the warm breeze and an old-fashioned gas pump looks ready to serve the next customer. Although Odell's Standard Oil Gas station (built in 1932) is no longer selling gasoline, it has become a welcome center for the Village of Odell. The station won the National Historic Route 66 Federation Cyrus Avery Award in 2002 for the year's most outstanding Route 66 preservation project. The historic station is located at 400 S. West Street.

Figure 117the design of the Odell gas station is similar to the majority
of station designs in the 1930s like this restored Sinclair station built in 1928

Gardner, Illinois

The village of Gardner, Illinois (population-1,500) has preserved many Route 66 related attractions of which the Riviera Roadhouse takes center stage as being gangster Al Capone's hangout.

The Riviera Roadhouse in Gardner has a fascinating history. Jack Rittenhouse mentions it in his guide book as being at the intersection of the road into Gardner and Route 66. The Riviera Restaurant and Tavern was built in 1928. James Girot, a South Wilmington businessman, moved buildings from Gardner and South Wilmington and put them all together to form the Riviera structure as it stands today. The Riviera is a true roadhouse! Once movie legends Gene Kelly and Tom Mix regularly stopped here. This was a favorite haunt of Al Capone and was known as a gangster hangout too. Slot machines and booze were offered to the discrete customer during prohibition. In fact, there's a freezer in the basement with a heavy iron door that was used to hide booze and gambling machines in case of a raid.

Figure 119 Bob Kraft, owner of the Riviera tells stories of its checkered past

Figure 118 the Riviera burns in 2009 after Bob Kraft retired

Figure 120 this was the casino area of the Riviera when Capone visited. Now used for special events

When Bob Kraft and his wife Peggy decided to retire in 2008 they sold the business and the property. The next year a fateful fire ended the historic heritage of the Riviera Roadhouse but the fire did spare a wonderful "Route 66 Diner" that was located several yards away.

The streetcar is over one hundred years old and yes, it truly was a horse drawn streetcar.

Purchased in 1932 with the intention of converting it into a roadside diner and moved the streetcar to Gardner. This was a no-frills operation, simple and to the point. A small sign on the exterior identified it as a diner, and its reputation for good food.. For a while it was even used as an unofficial bus stop for the Greyhound line.

Figure 121 Route 66 Diner interior

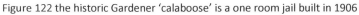
Figure 122 the historic Gardener 'calaboose' is a one room jail built in 1906

After the Riviera fire, there's been talk about moving the street car/diner to a protected area alongside of the historic Gardener jail. So if you go to the Riviera site and it's not there, go here: E. Mazon St., Gardner, IL Take I-55 exit 227. Drive east for about a mile on Main St. Turn left onto Center St., then make the second right onto Mazon St.

CHAPTER
FIFTEEN

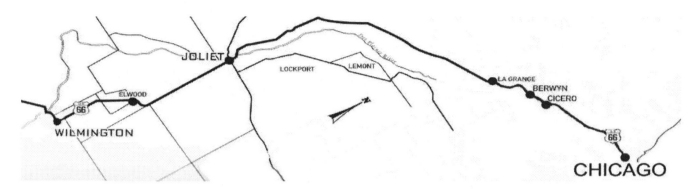

As you've probably noticed by now, this is not a book for tourists but a book for Route 66 *travelers*-people who aren't afraid to take a side-road without knowing where it leads -folks who will travel thousands of miles for the adventure of driving an unpredictable car like the English Austin 7, from New Jersey to California and along the full length of Route 66.

Richard and Marlies Bishop with their 1938 Special.

Peter Peeters and Adriana with the oldest car, a 1926 "Chummy."

George and Joy Mooney with our 1934 Cambridge Special

Geoff Cox with his Box Saloon.

The "crew" as they like to call themselves, are members of the British 750 Motor Club. Their friend, and fellow club member Ron Garside, always dreamed about Driving Route 66 but died before he could do so. His family, friends and fellow club members decided to drive '66' in his honor and memory. They shipped their cars to Newark, New Jersey and drove them to Chicago for their first leg of the journey. The caravan of classic cars planned to drive 180 miles a day at an average speed of 45 mph (about max for these little cars) and hoped to complete their journey in about a month.

The first record of an Austin 7 driving the length of Route 66 was back in 1946 (when the road was in good repair) when Jack Rittenhouse drove his 1939 Austin Bantam on 'The Mother Road.' Jack ended-up writing about his travels in his book: *A Guidebook To Highway 66*.

Joliet, Illinois
Route 66 Raceway

The 250-acre facility was built in 1998, funded by nine local entrepreneurs headed by Dale Coyne. The inaugural season saw 90 days of racing activity. In 1999, ISC partnered with the founders of the facility when it purchased 930 acres of land adjacent to the facility to build Chicagoland Speedway.

The quarter-mile, $20 million drag strip features a four-story, 38-suite complex. The 30,000-seat grandstand surrounds the start line and features rows of fully backed seats. In 2010, the drag strip was repaved.

Past events on the half-mile dirt track have included World of Outlaws sprint cars, late models, and monster truck shows. In recent years the oval has been used exclusively for Team Demolition Derby's , as well as TORC: The Off Road Championship.

The adjacent Chicagoland Speedway holds dirt track and full NASCAR races. Both are wonderful to see but the traffic in-and-out can be horrendous.

Figure 123 trailer hides a major dragster

Figure 124 quarter-mile drag strip at 66 Raceway

Figure 125 bringing their car for an afternoon run

Chicago, Illinois

Well, you made it! To both the end and the beginning of the road! What you now need to complete your adventure is to find the Route 66 signs announcing both the beginning and end of 'The Mother Road' and then a good meal! I would suggest Lou Mitchell's as an icon of Route 66 food and an all around great place to eat. If you drive local '66' you absolutely *must* pay them a visit.

Jackson Boulevard was the starting point for the original Route 66, which means you can drive into Chicago on the 'Mother Road' from the Kennedy Expressway, Illinois Interstate 90/94. Exit Jackson east and look for Lou Mitchell's on your right located near the intersection of Jackson and Jefferson. You will find the signs nearby.

Figure 126 '66' begins

Figure 127 '66' ends

Figure 128 a happy couple ordering at Lou's

I hope that your trip was a personal 'journey of discovery' and you found the living history of what America once was, traveling the "Old Road." There are hundreds of towns and things to see out there, between Chicago and Los Angeles - and an historic road that knows just where they all are. Each town and each person you meet along Route 66 has a story to tell. Take the time to hear what that story is. After all, like I said earlier, it's the journey not the destination that drew you to Route 66 in the first place.

Figure 129 Blue Highway - by Joseph Caro

Figure 130 "66' Night Storm' by Joe Caro

If you somehow find that your travels on Route 66 were memorable, I have two posters of Route 66 art you may find interesting, and they both are personally signed. Details about this *beautiful impressionistic art* (and several others) can be found on the book web page: cruisin-route-66.com

Chicago is not the end of my trip however, I must continue on. The British 750 Motor Club started their Route 66 adventure in New Jersey, so I am planning to end mine there. I will be heading to a small New Jersey town called Dunellen - for the best dang chili dog I've ever eaten! –It's called a "Texas Weiner." You can find me there. . . .*So saddle-up Pardner!*

Route 66 2016 Events

Google search ROUTE 66 EVENTS for details

-
-
- Jan. 1 — **Tournament of Roses Parade Pasadena, Calif.**
- March 19 — **Race to the Rocker from Cuba to Fanning, Mo.**
- April 28-30 — **A Gathering of Nations Pow Wow Albuquerque.**
- April 29-May 1 — **Arizona Historic Route 66 Fun Run.**
- May 7 — **El Reno Fried Onion Burger Day Festival El Reno, Okla.**
- May 7-8 — **Route 66 Reunion, Albuquerque.**
- May 21 — **Clinton Route 66 Festival Clinton, Okla.**
- May 28 — **Bethany 66 Festival Bethany, Okla.**
- June 2-5 — **Rockabilly on the Route Tucumcari, N.M.**
- June 4 — **Route 66 Blowout Sapulpa, Okla.**
- June 4 — **Oklahoma Route 66 Corvette Roundup, Edmond, Okla.**
- June 4 — **World's Largest Calf Fry Festival & Cook-Off Vinita, Okla.**
- June 8-19 — **Mother Road Ride Rally**
- June 10-11 — **Edwardsville Route 66 Festival, Edwardsville, Ill.**
- June 10-12 — **Illinois Route 66 Motor Tour.**
- July 15-17 — **European Route 66 Festival Stuttgart, Germany**
- Aug. 12-14 — **Birthplace of Route 66 Festival Springfield, Mo.**
- Aug. 13 — **Oldham County Roundup Vega, Texas.**
- Aug. 24-27 — **Will Rogers Memorial Rodeo Vinita, Okla.**
- Sept. 23-24 — **Route 66 Cruisers Cruise-In & Car Show Claremore, Okla.**
- Sept. 23-25 — **International Route 66 Mother Road Festival Springfield, Ill.**
- Oct. 1 — **Oklahoma Czech Festival Yukon, Okla.**
- Oct. 8 — **Rendezvous Back to Route 66 San Bernardino, Calif.**
- Oct. 1-9 — **Albuquerque International Balloon Fiesta**
- Nov. 4-7 — **Will Rogers Days Claremore, Okla.**
- Nov. 10-13 — **Route 66 Festival, Los Angeles.**
- Nov. 19-20 — **Route 66 Marathon Tulsa.**

Made in the USA
San Bernardino, CA
19 March 2020